Ripley's Believe It or Not!

BOOK of the MILITARY

With Leonard R.N. Ashley

PUBLISHED BY POCKET BOOKS NEW YORK

Another *Original* publication of POCKET BOOKS

POCKET BOOKS, a Simon & Schuster division of
GULF & WESTERN CORPORATION
1230 Avenue of the Americas, New York, N.Y. 10020

Copyright © 1976 by Ripley International, Ltd.

Published by arrangement with Ripley International, Ltd.

ISBN: 0-671-82899-1

First Pocket Books printing June, 1976

10   9   8   7   6   5   4   3

Trademarks registered in the United States and other countries.

Printed in the U.S.A.

I am tired and sick of war. Its glory is all moonshine. . . . War is hell.

—General Sherman (1820–1891), 1879

Truly a Book to Amuse and Amaze!

Here are fascinating chronicles of incredible military oddities gathered from all over the world by the famous Ripley's team. This collection of little-known facts comes from the long history of men at war—and will cause disbelieving shakes of the head from the millions of Ripley's fans!

If you cannot find your favorite **Believe It or Not!** POCKET BOOK at your local newsstand, please write to the nearest Ripley's "Believe It or Not!" museum:

19 San Marco Avenue,
St. Augustine, Florida 32084

901 North Ocean Blvd.,
Myrtle Beach, South Carolina 29577

175 Jefferson Street,
San Francisco, California 94133

145 East Elkhorn Avenue,
Estes Park, Colorado 80517

Rebel Corners,
Gatlinburg, Tennessee 37738

1500 North Wells Street,
Chicago, Illinois 60610

4960 Clifton Hill,
Niagara Falls, Canada L2G 3N5

Boardwalk and Wicomico,
Ocean City, Maryland 21842

Ripley's Believe It or Not! titles

Ripley's Believe It or Not! 2nd Series
Ripley's Believe It or Not! 3rd Series
Ripley's Believe It or Not! 4th Series
Ripley's Believe It or Not! 5th Series
Ripley's Believe It or Not! 6th Series
Ripley's Believe It or Not! 7th Series
Ripley's Believe It or Not! 8th Series
Ripley's Believe It or Not! 9th Series
Ripley's Believe It or Not! 10th Series
Ripley's Believe It or Not! 11th Series
Ripley's Believe It or Not! 12th Series
Ripley's Believe It or Not! 13th Series
Ripley's Believe It or Not! 14th Series
Ripley's Believe It or Not! 15th Series
Ripley's Believe It or Not! 16th Series
Ripley's Believe It or Not! 17th Series
Ripley's Believe It or Not! 18th Series
Ripley's Believe It or Not! 19th Series
Ripley's Believe It or Not! 20th Series
Ripley's Believe It or Not! 21st Series
Ripley's Believe It or Not! 22nd Series
Ripley's Believe It or Not! 23rd Series
Ripley's Believe It or Not! 24th Series
Ripley's Believe It or Not! 25th Series
Ripley's Believe It or Not! 26th Series
Ripley's Believe It or Not! 27th Series
Ripley's Believe It or Not! 28th Series
Ripley's Believe It or Not! 29th Series
Ripley's Believe It or Not! 30th Series
Ripley's Believe It or Not! Anniversary Edition
Ripley's Believe It or Not! Book of Americana
Ripley's Believe It or Not! Book of the Military
Ripley's Believe It or Not! Book of Undersea Oddities
Ripley's Believe It or Not! Ghosts, Witches and ESP
Ripley's Believe It or Not! Stars, Space, and UFOs
Ripley's Believe It or Not! Tombstones and Graveyards

Published by POCKET BOOKS

Slogan for Victory

D-Day, the 6th of June 1944,
the massive invasion which
had been planned with clock-
work accuracy . . . down to the
designation of the official
military password . . . that
password was . . .
"Believe It or Not."

Returning in triumph to the
shores of the Philippines
General MacArthur spoke these
words: "Believe It or Not . . .
we are here."

August 8th, 1945 . . . the atom
bomb released over Nagasaki. . . .
At that crucial moment Captain
Behan, the bomber, uttered
these words: "Believe It
or Not . . . I've Got It."

BELIEVE IT OR NOT. . . .

Preface

War, said Heraclitus, is the father of everything. Of course, this is a generalization. But war is the basic subject of this book, and I have assembled here the most amusing and amazing facts from the long history of human conflict, documented from as far back as 1439 B.C. Undoubtedly, as Stanley Kubrick's *2001: A Space Odyssey* suggests, war emerged one dark prehistoric day when someone who had finished gnawing a bone suddenly realized that it, like a rock, could be used as a weapon.

This book is not intended to be an encyclopedia covering all aspects of war; rather, it is a collection of little-known facts—many of a bizarre nature—drawn from my own research and from the vast archives that the Ripley's BELIEVE IT OR NOT! team has built up in a long and distinguished career of cataloging the world's oddities. Mr. Ripley used to boast that he had a million researchers working for him. And indeed he did: those who followed his daily and weekly cartoons, syndicated in hundreds of newspapers throughout the world; those who listened to his radio programs; those who read his books; those who saw his early movies and television programs; and those who were fascinated by his museums of *curiosa,* collected from every corner of the globe. After researching this book, I've found that Dr. Samuel Johnson was speaking with typical British understatement when he said that "a man will turn over half a library to make one book."

In a book with so many facts, it would be vain to imagine that an occasional error has not crept in. But everything has been carefully checked and is *true*—BELIEVE IT OR NOT!

—L. R. N. ASHLEY
Professor of English
Brooklyn College of
the City University of New York

Ripley's Believe It or Not!®

BOOK
of the
MILITARY

Join the Army and Work in an Office

The United States spends as much for the military as China and Russia do combined. Most of it seems to be for the "administration," not the fighting forces.

In 1973 there were about one and a half million officers and non-commissioned officers in the United States Armed Forces—more admirals and captains, generals and colonels than there were at the height of World War II.

In that same year the United States had 42,000 military men in South Korea, 29,000 of them in offices. It was worse in Thailand: there were another 29,000 in offices out of the 36,000 stationed there. In the Philippines there were 11,000, out of a 16,000 total, in offices. It took 142,000 men and six billion dollars to train 221,000 inductees in 1973.

"Operating costs" constitute 70 percent of the current military budget. In 1974 Norman Cousins said, in *Saturday Review: World,* that "four out of every five military personnel are involved in desk work or noncombative functions."

Shower of Gold

The costliest bombardment of all time was a deadly shower of gold at Delhi in 1296.

In that year the Mohammedan conqueror, Allah-ud-din Khilji, invaded India and laid siege to Delhi. The siege was a protracted one. Inside, the defenders were running out of food and water. Outside, the attackers were running out of ammunition.

Finally, Allah-ud-din, ("The Beloved of God"), was advised by his generals that there were no more stones for his massive catapults. So near to victory, they would have to raise the siege.

Suddenly, Allah-ud-din had an idea. He gave instructions that the engines of war be loaded with 100-pound sacks of gold.

After several hundred "rounds" of this precious ammunition were showered on the city, Delhi surrendered and, it is presumed, Allah-ud-din got his money back. If each single round weighed 100 pounds, the cost of a bombardment of 100 rounds at current gold prices would be around a *hundred million dollars.*

THE ONE-EYED ARMY

You Can't Escape The Draft

Egyptian army life in the 1840s was pretty tough. So tough, in fact, that many men blinded themselves in one eye to escape conscription. Mohammed Ali, a common soldier who had risen to the rank of *Pasha,* was aware of such tricks. Consequently, he created two regiments of infantry consisting entirely of one-eyed soldiers. These units were maintained for more than 50 years. Mohammed Ali died insane in 1849, but his one-eyed soldiers went marching on.

"Fin de la guerre" (END OF THE WAR)

DURING THE SPANISH DUTCH WAR IN 1585-THE DUTCH BUILT A BATTLESHIP SO POWERFUL THEY THOUGHT IT WOULD END THE WAR—HENCE THE NAME "END OF THE WAR"

INSTEAD OF ENDING THE WAR— IT WAS SUNK IMMEDIATELY AND THE WAR CONTINUED FOR 63 YRS.

The BATTLE BETWEEN SPAIN AND ITALY THAT WAS WON BY--GREASE!

A SPANISH ARMY ASSAULTING the Italian island of Palmaria in 1494 TRIED FOR 8 HOURS WITHOUT SUCCESS TO CLIMB ITS ROCKY SLOPES -BECAUSE THE DEFENDERS HAD COATED THE CLIFFS WITH GREASE!

The Enemy Was Stoned

Rocks were surely among the first weapons used by man. In time, huge siege machines were invented to hurl them at the enemy and, eventually, cannons were used to fire stone balls. On one historic occasion, though, the most primitive method was used in the simplest but most devastating manner. It was on November, 15, 1315, at the Battle of Mortgarten that a Swiss force of only 1,500 pikemen and archers trapped an Austrian army of 8,000 men between a high mountain and a lake. They won the day by simply hurling boulders and trees down on them.

Pikers

The pike, cousin to the javelin and the lance, was used from medieval times right up to the present century.

In peacetime, when swords were beaten into ploughshares, pikes were used as barriers on toll roads—hence, the term "turnpike."

That's as plain as a pikestaff, isn't it? But why a miser or coward is called a "piker," nobody seems to know.

SHRAPNEL WAS INVENTED BY GENERAL HENRY SHRAPNEL – AND HE WAS THE FIRST MAN WOUNDED BY SHRAPNEL DUE TO A PREMATURE EXPLOSION IN 1793 AT THE EVACUATION OF DUNKIRK THIS EVACUATION WAS ASTOUNDINGLY SIMILAR TO THE DUNKIRK OF 1940

THE HORSE WAS THE FIRST SECRET WEAPON! ITS INTRODUCTION INTO WARFARE BY THE HITTITES GAVE THEM A WORLD EMPIRE!

The Soldiers Who Refused to Bite the Bullet

It was 1857. The British raj in India was at its height. The government declared that the 14-pound "Brown Bess" would be replaced by a lighter rifle, the new 8-pound, 14-ounce Enfield. The Enfield not only required a close-fitting cartridge and ball to be rammed down the 39-inch-long barrel, but the cartridges had to be greased as well. What mattered most to the Moslem soldiers was whether the cartridges, in their shiny yellow paper, were greased with mutton fat,

19

as ordered by Ordnance, or with cow or pig fat. The Moslems and Hindus were both forbidden by religion to bite off the end of a cartridge greased with fat that was, so to speak, "not kosher."

Lord Canning fumed. The cartridges could be torn with the left hand. Why all this nonsense? The custom seemed absurd to the Englishman. The military secretary, Colonel Richard Birch, didn't know (or perhaps didn't care) what kind of grease was used, but the commander-in-chief was a fierce old fogy named General George Anson. His attitude was: "I'll never give in to their beastly prejudices." He didn't even intend the pun.

On a Saturday in May 1857, 85 Indians of the Fourth Light Cavalry refused to bite the bullet. They would lose their caste by tasting cow or pig fat. They were all court-martialed and found guilty. Divisional Commander Major-General William Hewett disgraced the Sepoys by putting them in irons, stirring up talk of mutiny among them.

Mohun Lal, noticing that the Moslems were angrily sharpening their swords, informed his second-lieutenant of a possible attack. The second-lieutenant did not believe him. Lieutenant Hugh Gough, however, did believe him and reported the incipient mutiny to Colonel Carmichael Smyth. Smyth told him he "should be ashamed" at listening to such gossip. Gough then went to Brigadier Archdale Wilson, commandant of the station, who also pooh-poohed the potential mutiny.

The next day, Indian troopers in the bazaar were taunted by prostitutes for hanging around a brothel instead of helping their brothers in jail. Murder, arson, and looting broke out. People recalled that when Lord Canning, the new governor-general had arrived 14 months before, his stumbling on the red-carpeted stairs had looked like a bad omen for his regime. The prophecy of "All will be red" that had been circulating among the Indians was suddenly coming true.

The streets resounded with *Din! Din!* ("For the faith"), and *Allah-i-Allah maro Faringhi*. ("With the help of God we shall kill the Christians"). It was Holy War. The Indian army, with only 38,000 Europeans among the ranks of 238,000 men, was in mutiny. Meerut, where there were more Europeans than most places, was ravaged. Elsewhere, it was even worse.

Hugh Gough, the young lieutenant whose warning might have stopped the mutiny, was later knighted and became a general. But his greatest potential service to the army had been refused. Had the authorities listened to him, thousands of lives and millions of dollars in property might have been saved.

But, then, neither did anyone listen when it was predicted that Pearl Harbor would one day be attacked.

Dubious Achievements

In the "Dubious Achievements Awards" for 1967, *Esquire* Magazine cited the U.S.A.F. jets that attacked ten water buffalo, which were supposedly "heavily laden with what was suspected" to be enemy ammunition. There was no ammunition.

The prize probably ought to go elsewhere, however. What about the B-52 saturation bombing raid on a completely deserted Vietnamese village (no one was hurt and not one building was destroyed), which experts hailed as a great victory for "psychological purposes"? Or how about the President who expressed his determination "to keep fighting until the violence stops"?

Roderic ("The Elusive")

Roderic, the last Visigoth king of Spain was said to have been defeated by the Moors beside the river Guadalete in July of 711. But historians disagree as to whether he was killed in the battle, drowned after the battle—or whether he survived the battle and died two years later. *Some are not even sure that there was a battle!*

August II ("The Strong")

Soldiers are supposed to be a little bit wild on leave, but look at August II ("The Strong"), the battling king of Poland and Saxony. He lived from 1670 to 1733 and, between battles, he found time to father 355 children. Only one of them was legitimate. That child succeeded him as August III.

The Uniform

The earliest armies did not recognize themselves or their opponents by uniforms. Sometimes there was a uniformity of helmets and arms but, for the most part, each man provided himself with protective clothing as best he could.

It is said that military uniforms were created by Louis XIV (the Sun King) in 1668 so that the ladies— who preferred soldiers—could distinguish them from civilians.

The first uniforms were more elaborate than necessity demanded, and certain touches in those devised by Frederick the Great for his Prussian forces—such

THE *FIRST* ARMY UNIFORMS WERE WORN BY THE SOLDIERS OF LOUIS XIV IN 1668 IN ORDER THAT THE LADIES (WHO PREFERRED SOLDIERS) COULD DISTINGUISH THEM FROM CIVILIANS

as powdered hair—were copied by other forces, including the American troops of the Revolution. The British also powdered their hair, but they eventually had to give it up: the soldiers used flour for that purpose, and there was a shortage of that staple.

Some of the nineteenth-century uniforms of uhlans, dragoons, and other cavalrymen were unbelievably expensive and elaborate. Quite often, the original purpose of a style was lost and simply became a matter of fashion. An example of this was the uniform jacket of the Hussars. At first, it was slung casually over the shoulder, but later it became too small to wear any other way.

The buttons of some artillery regiments were of a dark material so that they would not betray snipers in the dark. However, most military buttons were made of bright brass until fairly modern times. This was another "bright" idea of Frederick the Great, who liked to see them sparkle as his troops marched by.

Again, it was Frederick who invented "grace buttons" that still appear on civilian suits. Buttons are no longer sewn on the cuffs of uniforms, but they did originally serve a purpose: to prevent common soldiers from wiping their noses on their sleeves!

At least in battle, modern officers' uniforms are more or less similar to those of their troops. It was discovered in World War I that it did not pay to dress officers in resplendent uniforms, not only because of all the mud and blood, but also because the enemy was quick to notice badges of rank and killed the officers first. Rank has its dangers as well as its privileges!

If Lord Nelson had not distinguished himself by wearing all his orders and decorations when on the deck of the *Victory* at the Battle of Trafalgar, snipers in the rigging of enemy ships might not have been able to single him out as a prime target.

For a long while, naval officers were permitted to design their own uniforms, as long as blue was featured in the ensemble. In time, sailors adopted distinctive straw hats with ribbons and pigtails. Trousers became bell-bottomed so that they could be more easily taken off in the water, or rolled up for swabbing the decks. As a result, they were nicknamed *swabbies*.

Military Sashes

The dark red military sashes so distinctive in British and American army uniforms of Revolutionary times were at one time very long. For example, the sash worn by General Edward Braddock in the 1755 battle against Daniel Beaujeu and his Indian and French allies was 11 feet long. In that battle, 63 of the 89 British officers were casualties; and Braddock, who had four horses shot from under him, died a few days later. On his deathbed he presented his military sash to George Washington, who was then serving under him in the king's forces.

Washington kept the sash as a souvenir and wore one like it when he fought the British 20 years later. However, Washington's was only 8 feet long.

Why the excessive length? Because the sash was more than an ornament; it could be strung up like a hammock to serve as a portable bed. Washington had no need for this, however, because he slept in a folding walnut camp bed that he took along everywhere.

Response

"A bad peace is even worse than war," wrote Tacitus in about A.D. 110.

"There never was a good war or a bad peace," wrote Benjamin Franklin in 1773.

Famous Last Words

Historians argue about what Nelson said when he was dying at the Battle of Trafalgar. Was it "Kismet, Hardy" or "Kiss me, Hardy"? Or, after three-and-a-quarter hours of suffering, did he die while repeating, "Thank God I have done my duty"?

Who's Right?

What are we supposed to do when military experts disagree?

Two Prussians who revolutionized the theory of war were diametrically opposed on basic strategy. Carl von Clausewitz (1780–1831) wrote: "The *defensive* form of war is itself stronger than the *offensive*." But Friedrich von Bernhardi (1849–1930) wrote: "The *offensive* is the stronger form of war, and has ever gained in superiority."

Who's right?

Clausewitz on Clausewitz

Carl von Clausewitz (1780–1831), who served importantly in Prussian and Russian armies, wrote even more importantly on war. His books revolutionized military strategy.

When he died at Breslau of cholera, his wife opened the sealed packets he had left and discovered that his great work was unfinished.

Disregarding the note found among his literary remains she published the manuscript. The note warned: "Should the work be interrupted by my death, then what is found can only be called a mass of conceptions not brought into form . . . open to endless misconceptions."

Does that fairly describe one of the classics of military writing?

The leading military writer, Captain B.H. Liddell Hart, in his book *Strategy,* claims that Clausewitz's concept of "total war" *was* misunderstood—a misinterpretation that resulted in World War I and that "all too logically, [led] to World War II."

GENERAL
CARL VON CLAUSEWITZ
AUTHOR OF "PRINCIPLES OF WAR" (WRITTEN IN 1810)
USED AS A TEXTBOOK FOR 130 YRS. BY THE GERMAN MILITARY MACHINE
AS THE INSPIRATION OF GERMAN MILITARISM, HE HAS CAUSED
MORE LOSS OF LIFE THAN ANY OTHER MAN
IN HISTORY

HANNIBAL GREATEST OF ALL GENERALS

FOUGHT CONTINUOUSLY FOR **15** YEARS - IN THE ENEMY COUNTRY — WITHOUT SUPPLIES FROM HOME — *WITHOUT LOSING a SINGLE Battle!*

HIS ARMY WAS ONLY **26,000** MEN — YET HE WON **1600** BATTLES *KILLING* **300,000** *ROMANS*

Cannae

Polybius wrote 40 history books (only five remain complete) to prove that Rome was destined to rule. But one of the events recorded by him was a tremendous setback for the power of Rome.

At Cannae in 216 B.C., the Romans put the largest army they ever massed into action. Hannibal trounced them, and the Romans lost 70,000 men in one of the greatest military massacres ever known.

The two Roman consuls had argued over strategy. Varro favored a head-on clash with Hannibal; he won the argument—and lost the battle. Ironically, he was one of the few who survived. Paullus, who had advocated caution, was killed.

What the Great Scholars Had to Say

The Romans who were supposed to know the most about war wrote the least about it. At least this was true of such famous men as Catullus, Horace, Juvenal, and Vergil:

Catullus (Gaius Valerius, c. 84–54 B.C.) was a soldier on the staff of Memmius, governor of Bythnia. *He wrote lyrics.*

Horace (Quintus Horatius Flaccus, 65–8 B.C.) was an officer in the army led by Brutus that Antony and Octavius defeated in Philippi in 42 B.C. *He also wrote lyrics.*

Juvenal (Decimus Junius Juvenalis, c. 60–140 A.D.) was disappointed in a military career. *He wrote satire.*

But Vergil (Publius Vergilius Maro, 70–19 B.C.) *was never a soldier.* His only known personal connection with war was when the political disorder caused by the Battle of Philippi led to the loss of his estate near Andes, close to Mantua. It was Vergil, however, who announced: *"Arma virorumque cano"* ("Arms and the man I sing") in his great literary masterpiece, the *Aeneid*. Based on Homer's folk epics, the *Illiad* and the *Odyssey,* Vergil's poem tells the tale of Aeneas, son of Prima, the defeated king of Troy in the Trojan War, and of three months in his busy life.

Vergil went to Greece to research his epic and died there, but was returned to Naples for burial. In his will, he ordered that the unfinished *Aeneid* be destroyed.

The Emperor Augustus overrode the author's last wish by publishing the epic. It has become one of the greatest treatments of "arms and the man" in all literature, the product of a scholar and a gentleman, *but not a soldier*.

The Study of Military History

"It can hurt no man to invent new policies and wisely to use the old."

So wrote Sir Richard Morysine (Morison), the man who, in 1539, dedicated to Henry VIII the first book printed in England on the art of war. The fact is, the man himself got all his knowledge from old books. He was certainly not knighted for services in the field—he never saw a battle.

"Light at the End of the Tunnel"

The war that probably did the greatest damage to the United States was Vietnam.

Dien Bien Phu fell on May 8, 1954. The French had already withdrawn, but that same year the United States was carrying 78 percent of the war in what was then called "Indochina." By 1957 the United States was paying for all of South Vietnam's military costs as well as about 80 percent of other government costs, plus nearly 90 percent of all her imports. At that time, the United States had only 16,000 "advisers" in Vietnam.

Ten years later, the United States Secretary of Defense told Congress that the United States would be out of Vietnam by the end of the year. But, at that time, United States bombing of North Vietnam had barely begun. General John D. Lavelle ordered unauthorized raids. The city of Hue was pulverized. President Johnson's "light at the end of the tunnel" remained remote.

The peak of the American military commitment to Vietnam came in April 1969, with a total force of 543,400 men. Mass anti-war demonstrations took place throughout the United States that year.

In the end, the United States pulled out its armed forces, in what was called "peace with honor." The cost? Over 100 billion dollars, 60,000 dead, and hundreds of thousands wounded.

Curtis Lemay's plan to "bomb them back to the stone age" had failed. The "doves" and the "nervous Nellies" had been right. BELIEVE IT OR NOT!, the United States had lost a war.

THE **WAR** THAT WAS WON BY AN ARMY OF TOY SOLDIERS!
KING DECEBALUS of Dacia (now Rumania),
HIS CAPITAL CITY OF SARMIZEGETHUSA BESIEGED BY AN
OVERWHELMINGLY SUPERIOR FORCE LED BY ROMAN GENERAL JULIAN,
TRICKED THE ENEMY INTO SURRENDERING TO AN ARMY OF PUPPETS
LONG A COLLECTOR OF PUPPET SOLDIERS, LIFE SIZE, AND ATTIRED
LIKE THE TROOPS OF DACIA, KING DECEBALUS HAD HUNDREDS OF
PUPPETEERS MANEUVER THE TOYS FROM THE WALLS OF THE CAPITAL.
*THE ROMANS PAID DACIA A FINANCIAL TRIBUTE ANNUALLY FOR
10 YEARS AS A RESULT OF THEIR HUMILIATING DEFEAT*

Boers or Boors

When the South African Boers fought the Germans in World War I, they refused to permit blacks in the forces. "The Government does not desire to avail itself of the services, in a combatant capacity, of citizens not of European descent," they said, "in a warfare against whites." These "undesirables" were allowed to perform only menial tasks.

When a black driver and his mule were killed, the owner of the mule was compensated by the government—but the driver was not even listed as a casualty.

All Wars Are Holy Wars

The Koran, sacred book of Islam, declares that war is both holy and necessary:

"When ye encounter the unbelievers, strike off their heads, until ye have made a great slaughter among them. Verily, if God pleased, He could take vengeance on them without your assistance, but He commandeth you to fight His battles."

—*Koran*, XLVII, C. 625.

The Soldier Emperors

One might be excused for thinking of some of the Roman emperors such as Heliogabalus or Nero as rather effeminate, but many of them were raised to that high office by the power of the Praetorian Guard and were soldiers of great courage.

Lucius Domitius Aurelianus succeeded Claudius II and reigned as the Emperor Aurelian for the last five

EMPEROR AURELIAN WHO RULED THE ROMAN WORLD FROM 270 TO 275, AS A SOLDIER BEFORE HE BECAME RULER **KILLED 950 ENEMIES IN HAND-TO-HAND COMBAT** *HE KILLED 48 SARMATIANS IN A SINGLE DAY'S BATTLE*

THE **VAGRANT WHO LED A ROMAN ARMY TO VICTORY!**

years of his hectic life. He eventually had to give in to the Gothic hordes, but he was able to consolidate the provinces along the Danube and hold the barbarians at bay behind the Rhine. His exploits in the East, where he captured Zenobia, were fabulous.

As one of the most active and aggressive of all the emperors of Rome, Aurelian established Roman sway in Britain, Gaul, Spain, Egypt, and Mesopotamia on a firm basis.

He built a wall 40 feet high and 12 miles long around Rome, parts of which stand to this day. However, his greatest achievements were as a soldier on the battlefield. Before he rose to the imperial purple, he had killed 950 enemies in hand-to-hand combat. In fact, Aurelian himself killed 48 Sarmatians in a single day's battle.

Another soldier emperor was, of course, Julius Caesar. He fought his own battles—and fought them very well—except once. On this single occasion, he was faced with a prophecy: "No Scipio will ever lose a war in Africa." His opponent that day was a man called Metellus Scipio. The Fates were denied when Caesar appointed, for that day only, a jobless civilian by the name of Cornelius Scipio to be commander-in-chief over all the Roman forces. Metellus Scipio was beaten and finally stabbed himself. The prophecy at least was half true. Cornelius Scipio won; Metellus Scipio lost.

Caesar then claimed command of the Roman forces once again.

The War of Jenkins' Ear

In 1731, shipmaster Robert Jenkins reported to the British authorities that his ship, *Rebecca,* had been boarded by Spanish coastguards off the West Indies, and that his ear had been cut off.

The story aroused no real interest in London, but several years later he was still telling his tale. In 1738, he related it to a committee of the House of Commons, presenting himself as an aggrieved hero who, in the moment of extremity, "committed my soul to God and my cause to my country."

Jenkins' speech helped those who were trying to arouse public opinion against the Spaniards. Tempers were inflamed. Debates erupted, and England was forced to declare war against Spain in October 1739.

The war came to be called "The War of Jenkins' Ear," but it was soon submerged in the hotter question of the War of the Spanish Succession. It did give Robert Jenkins, master mariner, his place in history—on the basis of a story that may not have even been true, for some claimed he lost his ear in an accident!

How Did the Conquerors Die?

Pedro de Valdivia, conqueror of Chile, was killed by Indians, as were Ponce de Leon (discoverer of Florida), Noblo de Chaves (conqueror of Bolivia), and Francisco Hernandez de Cordoba (discoverer of Yucatan and conqueror of the Mayans). Francisco Pizzaro and his half-brother Pedro de Alcantara, and Jorge Robedo (conqueror of Colombia) were all assassinated. Vasco Nunez de Balboa (discoverer of the Pacific) killed Diego de Almagro, and Diego's son killed him. Diego Centeno, Diege de Alvarado, and Diego de Ordaz were all poisoned. A horse fell on Pedro de Alvarado, fatally crushing him. Gonzalo Jiminez de Quesada (another conqueror of Colombia) died of leprosy at the age of 80. His brother was struck by lightning. Hernando Pizzaro (conqueror of Peru) was imprisoned in Spain, but at least he lived to be 104. Diego de Henares Lozana (a conqueror of Venezuela) lived to the ripe old age of 115.

The Crusaders

In 1095, Pope Urban II declared to the Council of Clermont that Christians should go to war for the Holy Sepulchre, which had been in the hands of the Moslems since the seventh century. As an incentive, he added that the journey to the Holy Land would count as full penance for all sins. The Moslems already believed in Holy War, but now the Christians also took up crosses, calling themselves *Crusaders*. Pope Urban also gave them their battle cry: *"Deus volt!"* ("God wills it!"). Well, Urban willed it, at least.

The Crusades are a long, fascinating story. Two groups of ill-assorted peasants marched ahead of the well-organized troops of the First Crusade. One group was led by *Gautier Sans-Avoir,* ("Walter the Havenot" or "Walter the Penniless"), and another by a poor preacher born in Amiens, *"Peter the Hermit."* Both groups, after incredible adventures—including lawlessness and looting—reached Constantinople.

Alexius I was Emperor of Byzantium. He was not exactly joyful at the arrival of these fierce mobs, but he gave them transport to Asia Minor. Once the Crusaders arrived, they were attacked—and almost annihilated—by the Seljuk Turks. "Walter the Penniless" was killed. "Peter the Hermit" escaped and returned to France. He founded a monastery and settled down peacefully, not exactly a "hermit," but certainly a man with a "low profile."

The saddest story is that of the Children's Crusade (1202–1204), led by the French peasant boy, Stephen of Cloyes. Seeing the earlier Crusades betrayed by venal grown-ups, an army of children set off for the Holy Land. Many never reached Marseilles. Others only made it as far as Italy. Those who survived were victimized by unscrupulous ship captains who sold them as slaves.

Even after nine Crusades (1095–1272), still more were advocated. But, at last, no one "crusading enough" —or childish enough—could be found to go.

THE GENERAL WHO WON HIS GREATEST VICTORY FROM HIS DEATHBED!

GENERAL FILIPPO SCOLARI, AN ITALIAN, WHO LED THE ARMIES OF EMPEROR SIGISMUND OF GERMANY, WAS SO FEARED THAT THE TURKS DELAYED AN INVASION OF GERMANY *UNTIL THEY RECEIVED A REPORT THAT SCOLARI HAD DIED*

THE REPORT WAS PREMATURE AND THE TURKS FLED IN CONFUSION WHEN SCOLARI, IN FULL ARMOR, WAS CARRIED ONTO THE FIELD OF BATTLE ON A STRETCHER *THE GENERAL DIED THAT VERY DAY!* (Dec. 27, 1426

You Gotta Have Faith

At one point during the Crusades, when the morale of the troops was at a low ebb, Peter Bartholomew, a monk from Marseilles, suddenly produced a spear, claiming that it had pierced the side of Jesus on the cross. Carrying the relic before them as a standard, the Crusaders marched on with renewed faith. When further encouragement was needed, Adhemar, a legate of the pope, called upon three knights from the hills. The men, dressed entirely in white, were introduced as St. Maurice, St. George, and St. Theodore, all martyrs for the faith. Inspired, the Crusaders again pushed on and won the battle.

Later, when some of the Crusaders doubted the authenticity of these miraculous things, Peter Bartholomew offered to run the gauntlet to prove the truth of his assertions. In an age when trial by combat was the rule, this seemed reasonable. He ran a gauntlet of fire and emerged apparently unscathed. Unfortunately, he died the very next day. Some said he died of burns; others claimed he had overtaxed his heart. For the Crusaders, however, faith in these divine aids was lost, and the "miraculous" spear was retired as a standard.

TALISMAN of CHARLEMAGNE

GREATEST RELIC IN THE WORLD CHARLEMAGNE WORE IT FOR 352 YRS. AFTER DEATH IT CONTAINS WOOD OF THE TRUE CROSS.

THE CRUSADES WERE THE RESULT OF THE TALISMAN

The Great Shah Abbas

Shah Abbas of Persia was a warlike man, encouraged in his ways by the arrival of two Englishmen to his land in 1598. Sir Anthony Sherley and his brother Robert brought information on casting cannon and other technology from the West. Soon Shah Abbas had muskets and 500 artillery pieces. With only 60,000 men, he was able to turn back 100,000 Turks and establish his rule.

Shah Abbas was a many-sided man. He built a gorgeous "Royal Square"—a vast rectangle surrounded by buildings—and was an early advocate of town planning. He killed one of his sons and blinded another—in spite of this, he was considered a cultivated man, a patron of the arts, and a philanthropist!

Though he never failed in military ventures, Shah Abbas was less successful when he tried to discourage his courtiers from smoking. He tricked them into filling their pipes with dried horse manure—but they liked it. It seems even the "Great Shah," himself, couldn't break the "nicotine habit." He could move a capital (as he did his, from Tabriz to Isphahan) more easily than he could move a confirmed tobacco smoker.

The Fauchers

The brothers Constantin and César Faucher had amazing careers. They were identical twins from La Réôle, in the Gironde, France.

They became lieutenants on the same day.

They became captains on the same day.

They became majors on the same day.

They became colonels on the same day.

They received identical wounds on the same battlefield.

They became brigadier generals on the same day.

They were tried and sentenced to death on the same day.

They were led to the guillotine together.

They were both reprieved at the last minute.

Their case was reconsidered. They were resentenced.

They were executed on the same day.

They looked so much alike that they could not be distinguished except by the different flowers they wore in their buttonholes.

"ONE FACE, ONE VOICE, ONE HABIT—BUT TWO PERSONS"

Constantin AND César Faucher

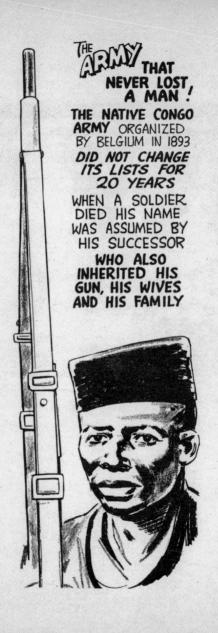

THE ARMY THAT NEVER LOST, A MAN!

THE NATIVE CONGO ARMY ORGANIZED BY BELGIUM IN 1893

DID NOT CHANGE ITS LISTS FOR 20 YEARS

WHEN A SOLDIER DIED HIS NAME WAS ASSUMED BY HIS SUCCESSOR

WHO ALSO INHERITED HIS GUN, HIS WIVES AND HIS FAMILY

The Fighting Irish

In addition to all those brave men with Irish names in British, Irish, and American forces, consider these:

Pierre, Count Lacy (1678–1751) was a Russian field marshal, born in Limerick, Ireland. He fought in the service of France before joining the Russian army at the age of 20.

Marie Edme Patrice Maurice MacMahon (1808–1893), marshal of France and president of the French Republic, was of Irish Jacobite descent.

Leopold O'Donnell (1809–1867), marshal of Spain, duke of Tetuen (Morocco), came from an Irish family.

Bernardo O'Higgins (1778–1842), hero of Chile, was the natural son of Ambrosio O'Higgins, Spanish viceroy of Chile and Peru.

Daniel O'Mahony, who held French commands under Villeroy and Vendôme, also led dragoons for the Spanish at Almanza.

Charles O'Brien, the French *maréchal-de-camp* who fell at Ramilles, had a son of the same name who was an officer in the French army. He fought with distinction at Dettingen and Fontenoy, becoming a marshal of France before he died at Montpelier.

The Luckiest Soldier in All History!

The luckiest soldier in all history was probably Field Marshal Lord John, first earl of Ligonier, born at Castres of Huguenot parents in 1697. He served for 61 years in the British army. He was made commander-in-chief in 1757 and a field marshal in 1766. As commander of a great regiment of Irish dragoons, he served at Fontenoy in 1745; but the highlight of his career was at the Battle of Malplaquet. On September 11, 1709, serving under the great duke of Marlborough, he was shot 23 times—yet he escaped without a scratch. All 23 bullets penetrated his clothing without hitting his body!

His varied and exciting career earned him the high honor of burial among England's heroes in Westminster Abbey.

THE LUCKIEST SOLDIER IN ALL HISTORY!
FIELD MARSHAL LORD JOHN LIGONIER (1680-1770)

Gordon of Khartoum

Charles George Gordon (1833–1885) was a religious fanatic whose most startling encounters were with other religious fanatics.

He acquired the nickname "Chinese" Gordon from the 33 battles his "Ever Victorious Army" fought against the *Taiping* ("Heavenly Peace") forces in China.

In 1837, a village schoolmaster in China named Hung Siu-tsuen experienced a religious vision in which he saw himself as *Tien Wang* ("Celestial King"), the younger brother of Jesus Christ. He then resolved to conquer all the "demons" in China.

Before Hung and Gordon were finished, nearly 30,000,000 lives had been lost.

It was another religious maniac, Mehemet Achmed, who called himself the Mahdi ("Messiah"), who finished Gordon. Gordon's incredible bravery and determination were not enough against the Mahdi; nor did consultation with his Bible (which wound up in a glass case in Queen Victoria's home) help him. It was foretold that the "Messiah" would meet Gordon face to face and that Gordon would die. However, it did not exactly happen that way.

Gordon was indeed killed (on the steps of the palace at Khartoum), but only after he was dead did they meet "face to face." Gordon's severed head was brought to the Mahdi at Omdurman and, after gloating over it, Mahdi hung it in a tree by the highway so that passersby could fling rocks at it.

This vulgarity caused "grief inexpressible" for Queen Victoria. "Indeed, it made me ill," she wrote. It also infuriated the British army into retaliation in the Sudan.

Within six months, the Mahdi died and, after thirteen years, his influence was finally erased.

Gordon's death prompted the action he had demanded—but had never received—while he was alive.

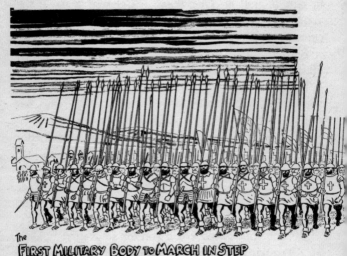

The FIRST MILITARY BODY to MARCH IN STEP WERE THE FAMOUS SWISS PIKEMEN OF THE 15TH CENTURY

UNLESS THEY KEPT IN STEP THEY COULD NOT CARRY THEIR 18-FOOT PIKES WITHOUT RUNNING INTO ONE ANOTHER.

All The Infantries in the World are Still Following their Example

Death March

The craziest command ever received by troops was given by Paul (1754–1801), second son of Peter III and Catherine II of Russia. His father's murder and his mother's lack of affection accounted for his bad temper; and he was inclined to what was politely called around the Russian court, "vexatious regulations." When he wasn't within earshot, he was called the "Mad Czar."

Probably the wildest of his sudden and inexplicable caprices occurred on a cold morning in 1799. The pedantic military maniac was reviewing his troops with his usual critical eye when he noticed that a button was missing from a soldier's uniform. He flew into a rage.

"About-face, march!" he ordered his troops, wanting to banish the offending rabble from his sight.

"Where to, Your Imperial Majesty?" he was asked.

"To Siberia!" he snapped.

And off they went. Without a murmur, 400 men, the pick of the guard, set off on the 2,000-mile trek to the snowy wastes of northern Russia. No food, no supplies, no good-byes. They had their orders! One hopes that, once out of sight, they deserted. But, more likely, they did not. No one knows. They were never seen again.

Years later, Paul died, never having cared what happened to his forsaken troops. He died in a scuffle when his own officers tried to compel him to abdicate.

The Arms Race

International trade in non-nuclear arms in 1975 ran around $20 billion—550 percent more than the amount spent ten years earlier. The major importer of arms in the world was Iran. The United States was the biggest exporter, selling or giving away $86 billion in the period from 1950 to 1975. The Soviet Union was a distant second: $39 billion in the same period. In 1974, the Soviet Union exported more supersonic aircraft than the United States (400 versus 325), but the Americans led with 100 helicopters and 1,177 tanks. After the 1973 war, Israel received more than $2 billion worth of United States weapons within two years—which left the United States National Guard and Reserve short of tanks. The Israeli arms bill for 1975 exceeded that figure in a single year. At the same time, Israel manufactures and exports more than $50 million in arms itself.

"July 14th; Nothing"

On the morning of July 14, 1789, 8,000 Parisians attacked the Hotel des Invalides. They captured 32,000 muskets and 12 pieces of artillery. Then someone shouted, "To the Bastille!" Apparently, the purpose was to get ammunition and powder rather than to free the half-dozen political prisoners held there (at least one of the prisoners had his own grand piano).

The mob stormed the ancient fortress. They lost 98 men, while the defenders, composed of French soldiers and Swiss Guards, lost only one. At last the fortress was surrendered. The mob then killed six defenders and, with the commander's head stuck on a pike, they marched through Paris.

The French Revolution had begun. Louis XVI cried, "This is a revolt!"

"No, Sire," responded the Duc de la Rochefeucauld-Liancourt. "It is a revolution!"

That morning the king had returned from hunting and had written in his diary at Versailles: "July 14th; Nothing."

What A Way to Go!

Some Russians thought that Grigori Yefimevich Rasputin's influence over the superstitious czarina interfered with ending the war for Russia. Several aristocrats—among them was Prince Yussupov, a lordling married to the czar's niece—decided to take matters into their own hands.

The result was the murder of Rasputin, "The Mad Monk"—which was accomplished by poisoning him, then shooting him, then beating him with sticks, and finally drowning him in a frozen river! According to Trotsky, it was carried out "in the manner of a moving-picture scenario designed for people of bad taste."

The story became the subject of the German film *Rasputin* (starring Conrad Veidt in 1930). The American version was *Rasputin and the Empress* (with Lionel Barrymore, 1932); the French, *Rasputin* (with Harry Bauer, 1938); the Italian, *Nights of Rasputin* (with Edmund Purdom, 1960); and the British, *Rasputin, the Mad Monk* (with Christopher Lee, 1966).

Oddly enough, when a film portrayed him as a murderer, Prince Yussupov, who had boasted of his part in the deed as a service to Russia, sued for defamation of character—and won. However, as late as 1968,

53

he was still being portrayed on the screen as the prime mover in the plot to rid Russia of the villain who, by treating the czarevich's hemophilia by hypnosis, was able to dominate the czarina, Czar Nicholas II, and Russia itself.

But even that is not the end of the grisly murder. In the 1917 February Revolution, Rasputin's poisoned, shot, beaten, and drowned corpse was dug up by the mob and burned.

Had the Russian mob thought of it, there was one more indignity they might have heaped upon him, even after all this. Returning to the days of Czar Peodor and his half-brother Dmitri, which signaled the end of Ivan the Terrible's dynasty, we can find yet another method of Russian contempt. Boris Gudenov (now remembered principally because of an opera based on his life) had secretly murdered Dmitri to clear his way to the throne, but Boris himself was becoming "terrible." His opponents, therefore, produced a false Dmitri, who claimed to be the surviving child of Ivan. When Boris died in April 1605, this new Dmitri entered Moscow in state and was crowned czar, but those who had disposed of the real Dmitri marched on Moscow and killed the imposter. They burned his body, filled a cannon with his ashes, and fired his remains in the direction of Lithuania, whence he had come.

The Dragoon in Drag

Charles d'Eon de Beaumont was born in Burgundy in 1728. He had one of the most controversial careers of all time. In an age when the governor of New York State went around in women's clothes and had his official portrait painted with himself dressed as a fine lady, even the Chevalier d'Eon caused talk.

As an officer of dragoons and aide-de-camp to Marshal Broglie, Charles risked his life at the Battle of Hoxten to rescue 400,000 cartridges that were under enemy fire. *But was he a man—or was she a woman?*

Chevalier d'Eon had been involved with diplomacy at the court of the Czarina Elizabeth on behalf of Louis XV. Having spent most of his life in England, he (or she) was in London in 1762, negotiating a part of the Peace of Paris. By 1771, bets began to be made about the chevalier's sex. Princess Dashkov from St. Petersburg pointed out that when the chevalier was in Russia, he was in long skirts. That was the way the Russian empress remembered him. Small (five feet four inches) and somewhat effeminate (some Englishmen said, "he's just French"), he did have a black beard. But was it real? Or was he a bearded lady?

Some £300,000 (an incredible sum in those days) was wagered in England alone on the chevalier's sex. The Court of the King's Bench tried cases about whether the wagers had to be paid off and who was to win; but it could not ask the chevalier (who had returned to France in a dress) to provide proof one way or the other.

In France, King Louis issued this official order: "Charles Genevieve Louise Augusta Timothee d'Eon de Beaumont is hereby commanded to lay aside the uniform of a dragoon, which he had been in the habit of affecting, and resume the garments of her sex; and is forbidden to appear in any part of our kingdom in any other garments than those suitable to a female."

A lady-in-waiting at Versailles planned a complete and expensive wardrobe for the new lady of fashion. And Mlle. d'Eon moved in with her mother in her native town of Tonnerre, a quiet backwater.

Later she moved back to England, spending the last 26 years of her eventful life there. She put on fencing

55

matches before the prince of Wales, but she fenced in petticoats. Wounded in one match, she retired in August 1796.

On May 22, 1810, the little old lady known to all London, on whose sex so much money had been wagered, passed on.

At that time, "the nice problem for history" (as Voltaire put it) was finally and unequivocally solved. The physical evidence proved the dragoon had been in drag; the Chevalier d'Eon was a man!

THE SEXSATIONAL Chevalier D'Eon -of FRANCE $2,000,000 WAS WAGERED ON WHETHER THIS PERSON WAS A MAN OR WOMAN!

THE CORPSE THAT RODE HORSEBACK FOR 500 MILES!
THE MARQUIS OF PONTLEZ of Quemeneven, France,
BANISHED FROM HIS COUNTRY AND FORCED TO
FIGHT INFIDELS IN THE HOLY LAND FOR 17 YEARS TO
ATONE FOR A SLAYING, CAME HOME TO DIE-
AT MARSEILLE HIS COMPANIONS PROPPED HIM IN HIS
SADDLE IN FULL ARMOR, AND ALTHOUGH HE DIED THE NEXT DAY,
HIS HORSE CARRIED HIM ACROSS FRANCE TO HIS OWN TOWN
THE CORPSE FELL FROM THE SADDLE IN FRONT OF HIS OWN CASTLE
-AND THE MARQUIS WAS BURIED THERE WHERE HIS HORSE HALTED
1355

Congratulate the Lady

In 1847 Jane Townsend was awarded the General
Service Medal of the British navy for her services at
Trafalgar, thus becoming the first Englishwoman ever
to receive a military medal. The first British woman
to be awarded an Order—outside of royalty and other
special women—was Cecilia Frances, Lady Northcote
who, in the New Year's Honours list of 1878, was
awarded the Imperial Order of the Crown of India.

57

Admiral King

Ernest Joseph King (1878–1956) attained the highest rank (five-star admiral) in the United States Navy. He was awarded the Distinguished Service Medal by the United States and also wore orders from Brazil, China, Cuba, Ecuador, France, Britain, Greece, Monaco, and Panama; but he never won his country's highest decoration—the Medal of Honor.

Like Topsy, it Jest Growed

Only 40 years ago, the United States Army was rated the sixteenth largest in the world—smaller than Romania's.

An Award for Disobedience

Some European orders are very odd. The Czech Order of the White Lion was first introduced in 1922 —but Czechs were *excluded* from receiving it. To wear the Danish Order of the Elephant you have to be a Protestant. Foreign members are not counted in the categories of the French *Legion d'Honneur,* which are restricted to 80 grand crosses, 1,000 commanders, and so on. The Premier Order of the Kingdom of Portugal is only awarded to Roman Catholics. So was the Golden Fleece.

The Order of Alfonso XII of Spain was founded in 1902, but it was renamed the Order of Alfonso X the Wise in 1939. The Prussian orders were those of the Red Eagle and the Black Eagle, and the one for merit had a French (not German) name: *Order pour la Merite.* The latter was created by Frederick the Great in 1740 to replace the Order of Generosity of Brandenburg which, curiously, was both military and civil.

But surely the most remarkable of all these was the Austrian Order of Maria Theresa, founded in 1757. It was the highest Austrian military decoration, and yet few of Austria's great generals could wear it. It was a distinguished award for disobedience!

To win the Order of Maria Theresa during the 161 years that it was so coveted, one had to be an officer who won a battle by flying in the face of orders.

An order for disobeying orders!

The DISTINGUISHED ORDER OF DISOBEDIENCE HIGHEST AUSTRIAN MILITARY DECORATION WAS THE ORDER OF *MARIA THERESA* - WHICH FOR 161 YRS. COULD BE AWARDED ONLY TO AN OFFICER WHO WON A BATTLE BY DISOBEDIENCE

THE **ORDER** of the **PURPLE HEART** CREATED BY GEORGE WASHINGTON In 1782 WAS BESTOWED ONLY 3 TIMES IN THE NEXT 150 YEARS -EACH TIME ON A SOLDIER FROM CONNECTICUT

The Cheapest and Highest Award

Some awards for valor have been very inexpensive; for instance, the victor's simple wreath of laurel leaves. But, for modern times, the Victoria Cross, the highest British award for bravery in action, gets the prize.

While most decorations are made of precious metal —generally silver or gold——the Victoria Cross is made of old cannons that were captured at the Battle of Sebastopol. It outranks all those elaborate and bejeweled orders and decorations, and even its ribbon is a simple purplish color, not a rainbow stripe like most.

Other awards carry titles and riches with them. The Victoria Cross brings the winner (assuming it is not received posthumously) an annual payment of £10 (under $25) for those below commissioned rank. Those who have won it twice (V.C. and Bar), get another £5 a year. If the recipient needs real financial help, the grateful nation will go as high as £75 a year. In addition, the V.C. winner gets 6d. a day, *whether he needs it or not,* which ought to buy him a couple of cigarettes—if he wishes to risk his life further by smoking.

Of course, by the time you read this, things may have changed. In the light of rising prices and inflation, the British government may have even doubled or tripled the money that goes with this coveted decoration. It certainly wouldn't cost them much; since the V.C. was instituted in 1856, only three men have won it twice (which is a better record, however, than the queen's Fire Service Medal for Gallantry, which has *never* been awarded since its foundation more than 20 years ago!).

If one wanted to sell a V.C. at an auction, collectors would probably pay more for the medal than the recipient would receive in annuities and pensions from it in an average lifetime. At an auction in London in 1964, a Manchester regiment paid £1,150 for the medal that Lieutenant William Thomas Forshaw had won with great gallantry in "The Vineyard" at Gallipoli in August 1915. In 1967, a V.C. (for which an American had offered £3,000) was given by the hero's widow to his squadron of the Royal Air Force. Sergeant John Hannah had won it in the air over Antwerp in September 1940, when he was only 18 years old—the youngest V.C. of World War II.

Hospital apprentice Arthur Fitzgibbon won a V.C. in 1860 at the age of 15. That medal, if it were for sale, or those of Surgeon-Captain Arthur Martin-Leake (1874–1953) and Captain Noel Godfrey Chavasse (1884–1917) won in World War I, would undoubtedly bring a fortune.

MATHILDA NEWPORT, an aged crone, BECAME FAMED AS "THE JOAN OF ARC OF LIBERIA" WHEN SHE SAVED THE SEAPORT CITY OF MONROVIA BY LIGHTING THE POWDER OF AN ABANDONED CANNON WITH HER CORN COB PIPE THE ENEMY FORCES FLED AND THE CITY'S DEFENDERS RETURNED TO THEIR POSTS (Dec 1, 1822)

Oldest Social Club in North America

You can still become a member of an organization that was founded in 1606 to cheer up the soldiers of a French commandant.

There are no meetings of the club, no dues, and no qualifications demanded of members except that they vacation in Nova Scotia. Consult the Nova Scotia tourist authorities next time you are planning to visit that maritime province of Canada. The organization, called in English "The Order of the Good Time," was founded by Samuel de Champlain (1567–1635), explorer and founder of Quebec.

The First Campaign Medal

The Battle of Dunbar in the English Civil War is not remembered much today, and yet it has a great distinction: to commemorate it, the Parliamentary Army struck and issued the very first campaign medal in 1650. Prior to this date, only a few medals had been struck to commemorate such events as the defeat of the Spanish Armada.

ANGÉLIQUE BRULON (1771 - 1859)
- FEMALE LIEUTENANT AND FIRST WOMAN TO BE DECORATED
WITH THE LEGION OF HONOR —

The First Woman to Receive the **Legion D'Honneur**

The principal order of republican France is the *Legion of Honor,* founded by Napoleon in 1802. Few have done more to win it than Angélique Brulon (born in 1771), the first woman to be awarded that high honor.

She held seven ranks in the French army over a period of seven years. She took part in seven campaigns and was wounded seven times. She won seven decorations for bravery. She killed seven enemy soldiers. And she had seven children.

That's seven times seven.

She died in 1859 after living in an old soldiers' home for 60 years.

Horsemeat and Breastplates, Served With Panache

"An army," Napoleon said, "marches on its stomach" and, over the centuries, many incredible stories involving the feeding of armies have been recorded. Here are just two battlefield stories of French *cuisine,* both from the time of Napoleon.

After the Battle of Eylau, isolated on the Island of Lobau, Baron Larrey had his soldiers fed on soup made from horsemeat and the boiled breastplates of the cavalry. The soldiers seasoned their meat with gunpowder! Larrey had the forethought to put aside a little salt for himself, so he was able to invite Marshal Massena to a slightly tastier meal of *cheval.*

Necessity was again the "Mother of Invention" in June 1800, when shortages of food developed after the Battle of Marengo. Napoleon, who had not eaten all day, called for his dinner, and all that his chef, Dunand, had on hand were six crayfish, four tomatoes, three eggs, a small hen, oil, and garlic. The chef made a *panade* with the oil and his own ration of bread, browned the chicken, fried the eggs, tossed in the tomatoes and garlic, and steamed the crayfish on top of it all. He served it with *panache* ("a flourish") and a sauce.

"You must feed me like this after every battle," said the little corporal. *Chicken Marengo,* a version of *chicken Provençale,* had been created.

Later, Dunand took out the crayfish and put mushrooms into the recipe. He also substituted wine for the water, but Napoleon refused to eat it because he believed that changing the recipe would bring bad luck.

66

Today *chicken Marengo* is often made with mushrooms rather than crayfish. If it is served to you—refuse it.

You don't want bad luck, do you?

Volley

Concentrated firepower has always been the military man's dream. While the benefactor of humanity tries to make two blades of grass grow where only one grew before, the soldier wants to fire two missiles where only one was fired before; to fire more and faster, to get there the "fastest with the mostest," as an American general once said.

From ancient times, what we might call multiple weapons have been in common use. It may have been a sling that fired several projectiles at once; or it may have been the chariot of Boadicea, which not only got soldiers right into the thick of the action but, with

THE 1ST ARTILLERY VOLLEY
A MULTIPLE CROSSBOW
USED BY EUROPEAN
KNIGHTS IN THE 12th CENTURY
CONSISTED OF A CIRCULAR
ARRANGEMENT OF 4 CROSSBOWS
CAPABLE OF FIRING 12
ARROWS SIMULTANEOUSLY
IN 4 DIFFERENT DIRECTIONS
THE BOWS WERE OPERATED
BY A SINGLE WINDLASS

whirling scythe blades attached to the wheels, accomplished a lot of destruction in the process.

European knights in the twelfth century used a multiple crossbow which, when wound up with a single crank, was capable of firing four crossbows—a total of 12 bolts—in four different directions simultaneously. You just had to remember to lift it above your own head before pulling the trigger.

Batteries of cannons fired in succession was the next step and—at last—the repeating gun, which could spout bullets at a terrific rate.

The precursor of the modern machine gun was developed by an agricultural-machinery manufacturer and medical student, Richard Jordan Gatling, who was born in Winston, North Carolina, in 1818. Though born a Southerner, he was brought up in Indiana and Ohio, and it was to the North that he offered his Gatling gun in the Civil War. It was successfully demonstrated before the end of 1862, but the Ordinance Department did not get around to accepting it until 1866, by which time the Civil War was over.

Gatling's name turns up in poetry:

The gatling's jammed, and the colonel's dead,
And the regiment's brind with dust and smoke . . .

And at one time, every hard detective story had a gangster with an automatic pistol that was referred to as a "Gat" (derived from Gatling). The Marx Brothers used to pull out little guns and joke: "This Gat had gittons. . . ."

Another American invented the Maxim gun, but the machine was manufactured in Britain, and was first used by the Germans in World War I.

Sir Hiram Stephens Maxim was born in 1840 near Sangerville, Maine. He inherited the Yankee trait of

The
MAXIM
MACHINE GUNS

inventiveness and produced a number of clever devices before he went to England and invented the machine gun. Studying repeater-weapon designs, it occurred to him that the recoil from the explosion of one cartridge could be used to eject the empty shell and at the same time bring into place a new shell, thus reloading the weapon in an instant. The idea changed the face of warfare. In 1900, Maxim became a British subject and, in the following year, he was knighted for his services —which included the invention of smokeless powder, a delayed-action fuse, a heavier-than-air plane, and other aeronautical wonders of interest to him and his associates at the Vickers Company (later Vickers Armstrong Ltd.).

Sir Hiram's younger brother Hudson stayed in the United States, where he also contributed much to armament development with his high explosive (maximite), his smokeless powders (one of them stabilite), and his torpedo fuel (motorite). Sir Hiram's son Percy (1869–1936) developed the Maxim silencer for explosive weapons and other engineering marvels. However, it was Sir Hiram with his Maxim gun who was, to use the phrase his son chose as the title for his book, the *Genius in the Family*.

The First War Correspondent

When William Howard Russell's memorial was erected in St. Paul's Cathedral, the inscription described him as "The First and Greatest of War Correspondents." True, his reporting of the Crimean War for *The Times of London* made him famous, but those who remember Ernie Pyle, Winston Churchill, Ernest Hemingway, Edward R. Murrow, and a host of others may challenge Russell as "the greatest."

In any event, he was certainly not the "first." John Bell (editor of *The Oracle,* or *Bell's New World*) described the British battles from the front lines in Flanders at the end of the eighteenth century, and Henry Crabbe Robinson covered the Peninsular War in 1808 for *The Times.*

FASTER THAN SOUND!
THE "NAVY SKYROCKET"

Pliny

Gaius Plinius Secundus (A.D. 23–79), who was also called Pliny the Elder, wrote in his *Historia Naturalis* (A.D. 77) that, "as if to bring death upon man more swiftly, we have given wing to iron and taught it to fly." It sounds ominously like a prophecy of the aircraft and guided missiles of today.

72

The Uniform of the French National Guard

Charles Delahaye once played four sets of tennis in the uniform of the French national guard (wearing a field pack and carrying a musket with bayonet affixed). He beat his opponent, who was conventionally dressed—three sets to one.

Orville and Wilbur Wright Were Wrong

Orville and Wilbur were not exactly correct when they said they were the *first* to fly—and they do, indeed, deserve a lot of credit: for controlling the sustained power-driven flight and inaugurating the Age of Flight. But a monoplane "flew" with a young sailor aboard at Brest, France, about 1874. It had a hot-air engine, designed by Felix du Temple de la Croix. And Clement Ader flew his *Eole,* entirely under its own power, 164 feet at Armainvilliers, France, on October 9, 1890.

The Wright Brothers *were* right, however, when they said that flying was here to stay. Within about 20 years of their flight at Kitty Hawk, Orville lived (Wilbur died in 1912) to see two United States Army planes make the first flights around the world. It took only 57 "hops" and a mere 351 hours and 11 minutes of flying time. Orville was still alive when United States Air Force pilot Charles E. Yeager achieved the first supersonic flight in *Glamorous Glennis* at Edwards Air Force Base in October 1947.

FIRST WAR CORRESPONDENT
George Wilkins Kendall

REPORTED THE MEXICAN WAR (1846-7) FROM THE BATTLEFIELD EXCLUSIVELY FOR THE NEW ORLEANS PICAYUNE

— BY MEANS OF A SPECIAL PONY EXPRESS, HE WAS ABLE TO SCOOP ALL OTHER NEWSPAPERS — AND THE WAR DEPARTMENT AS WELL!

The Marquis de Lafayette

The Marquis de Lafayette's first name was Marie. So was his wife's.

74

On A Shoestring

When the Voisin brothers, Gabriel and Charles, set up the first factory in the world for the production of powered aircraft (Billancourt, 1906), they hired a boatbuilder and a carpenter to assist them. The men began work on an airplane with wings that flapped—but it never left the ground. With about five francs in the bank they kept working and, finally, in 1907, they came up with the first box-kite biplane, powered by a 50-hp. motor, and the aircraft industry had begun.

One, Two, Three—Fire!

The first hand grenades were used 800 years ago by the armies of the Caliph of Bagdad. They were pots filled with flaming petroleum that were flung at the enemy.

These first flame throwers were associated with what used to be called "Greek fire," but the idea obviously had its origins much further back in antiquity—perhaps as far back as the discovery of fire itself.

"Greek fire" was an inflammable mixture thought to have been composed of sulphur, naphtha, and quicklime. The Romans flung cauldrons of it at the walls of besieged citadels. The Byzantines fitted their ships with bronze tubes that spurted it at the enemy. In A.D. 673 and 718, they destroyed two Saracen fleets in a similar manner.

One historian says that the Greeks once set fire to ships at sea by reflecting the sun's rays from their highly polished shields ashore—and a modern experiment has proved this possible!

THE FIRST HAND GRENADES
WERE USED 800 YEARS AGO BY THE ARMIES OF THE CALIPH OF BAGDAD
THEY WERE POTS FILLED WITH FLAMING PETROLEUM AND FLUNG AT THE ENEMY

In the Middle Ages, castles were built to allow the defenders to pour boiling oil, burning pitch, or other nasty substances upon the heads of attackers.

The "tortoise" of linked Roman shields partially protected attackers from missiles such as rocks, arrows, and lances when they tried to undermine the walls of a stronghold—but it did not work exceptionally well against a torrent of hot lead or a curtain of fire raining down.

That was truly "working under fire"!

76

Grenadiers

The first regiment of foot guards in the British army, the Grenadier Guards, used to specialize in tossing hand grenades. Starting in the fifteenth century, a grenadier threw *grenades* (the French for "pomegranates") and, because they could see better, the tallest men were picked for this job. Regiments of all tall soldiers are still called Grenadier Guards, but they no longer specialize in this way.

Hand grenades regained their military popularity in the 1904–1905 Russo-Japanese War.

Dunkirk

Queen Victoria once said, "We are not interested in the possibilities of defeat." Over the centuries, however, the English, have been handed some very great defeats. In their inimitable way, they regard many of these as victories. One in particular was the heroic evacuation of British troops from Dunkirk, from May 29 to June 3, 1940, which poet laureate John Masefield immortalized in *The Nine Days' Wonder*. The history of that embattled town on the coast of France also records a *one day's wonder:* June 28, 1658. On that day, Dunkirk belonged to three different countries in a single 12–hour period. In the morning, it was Spanish; at noon, it surrendered to the French; and that evening, it was captured by the English.

8-7

DUNKIRK, the French city,
BELONGED TO 3 DIFFERENT COUNTRIES
IN A PERIOD OF 12 HOURS

Army Records

The largest armed forces in existence are probably those of China; the smallest, those of San Marino (11). The Swiss Guards, dating back to the fifteenth or sixteenth century, are the oldest.

Tiger Cages

In 1970 there was an international outcry over the "tiger cages" in which the Saigon government was holding some of its hundreds of thousands of war and political prisoners.

Saigon's reaction was to announce that the cages would be abandoned and, at the same time, they tried to force the prisoners themselves to build new cages—as a "self-help project." The prisoners refused, so new cages had to come from some other source.

On January 7, 1971, the United States Department of the Navy made a deal with an American company to build new cages for the Saigon government. The contract was for $400,000, and it paid for 384 new "isolation cells." However, when the prisoners were moved into the new "tiger cages," it was discovered that each unit had two square feet of space *less* than the old cages!

Pay Raise

In 1975 the 220,000 conscripts in the French army had their daily pay tripled. Before this, they had been collecting *60 cents a day* as privates.

RIPLEY AFTER F. PHILIPPOTEAUX

THE "BATTLE OF FONTENOY" — THE FAMOUS "BATTLE OF COURTESY"

"Gentlemen of the French Guard, Fire First!"

These words are perhaps the most famous in military history, but they were probably never said.

Voltaire was the creator of the legend that, at Fontenoy, in 1745, when Lord Charles Hay of the English First (Grenadier) Guards lined up his soldiers only 50 paces from the French, he shouted: "Gentlemen of the French Guard, fire first!", the French were supposed to have replied: "The French Guard *never* fires first."

The English fired first and, in one tremendous volley, they mowed down the first rank of French, killing more than 700 officers and men in an instant. The French Guard broke and ran. The English ran after them, 300 yards beyond the flanking batteries. The battle then turned in favor of the French, who eventually won the day.

Only one monument now stands on the field of Fontenoy. It honors neither the English nor the French. It was erected to the Irish forces who helped the French —and it refers to the English as "Perfidious Albion."

Jean Baptiste JOURDAN Marshal of France

The Inventor of Conscription

Jean Baptiste, Comte Jourdan, a marshal of France, was born in Limoges and scored great victories at Wattignies and Fleurus. In 1798 Jourdan introduced the first conscription law that made every Frenchman a soldier.

Napoleon made him a marshal and governor of Naples. Later, he left Napoleon to join the Bourbons, who made him a count but, in 1830, he switched again and supported the revolution.

Small Arms

Pizzaro launched the conquest of Peru with only two cannons.

The William Congreve Rocket

What would the famous English playwright, William Congreve, be doing in a book about the way of the military?

There was another William Congreve. Sir William Congreve (1772–1828) was an army officer, not a playwright and, in 1808, he invented the Congreve rocket. It had a range of about 1,500 yards and was notoriously unreliable. But the invention prompted the British army to form a new "Rocket Troop," and Congreve served as rocket artillery officer at Leipzig in 1813. Besides the war rocket, this ingenious man of science invented a time fuse, a parachute attachment for rockets, unforgeable bank-note paper, and fireworks.

Swords

Surrendering one's sword, or the breaking of a sword when a man is "drummed out" of the army, dates from the time when the sword was the mark of an officer and gentleman. Swords, now used only on ceremonial occasions, used to be a life-and-death matter. Their use in war goes back at least as far as the Assyrians.

The crescent design of the Moslem scimitar did not take its shape from the crescent moon of Islam as some have supposed, but had in its design more practical considerations. The Moslems at one time were supposed to have manufactured the very best swords, and they were surrounded by many legends. Among these was the one that the red-hot metal was tempered by being thrust through the body of some unfortunate prisoner or slave.

It is said that when Richard the Lion Hearted wanted to show Saladin the strength of Christianity, he placed an iron mace between two chairs and, with a single stroke of his great sword, cut it in half. Saladin then drew his more delicate scimitar, tossed a light silk handkerchief into the air and, as it fell, deftly cut it into many pieces. "This," he said, "is the subtlety of Islam."

Clothes Make the Man

The *cardigan sweater* and *raglan sleeves* on coats were both named after men connected with the Charge of the Light Brigade at Balaclava in 1854, one of the most heroic and useless episodes in English military history.

The Earl of Cardigan was in charge on the battlefield that day; and the first Baron Raglan was commanding the whole show in the Crimea, having succeeded Wellington (of the Wellington boots) as commander-in-chief.

Other articles of clothing named after well-known persons are the Eisenhower jacket and the Sam Browne belt, the latter invented in India in 1852. There are many others less well known such as the Spencer overcoat, named after the Earl of Spencer; the Dolly Varden hat; and the Tattersall vest.

Old Soldiers Do Die—
Privates Mostly

Sir Arthur Sloggett, who was shot through the heart at the Battle of Omdurman, lived for 31 more years, dying at the rank of general and the jolly old age of 72.

Some years ago the National Research Council in Washington did a study of 10,000 noncoms of World War II and discovered that death seems to respect rank, which does, after all, "have its privileges."

While more than 17 percent of the privates studied had "faded away" by the time the report was written, only 11 percent of the Pfc.'s, 9 percent of the corporals, and 8 percent of the sergeants had met their maker.

Foresight?

The Scottish inventor, Alexander John Forsyth (1769–1843), was the first to produce a workable percussion cap for the ignition of gunpowder in firearms.

Napoleon offered £20,000 for the invention—a fortune in those days—but Forsyth refused to reveal his secrets to the French, and settled instead for the small pension with which the British government later rewarded him.

More Morals, Please

The philosopher, William James, was no more war-minded than his novelist brother, Henry; but he argued that fighting gave scope to the heroic drives in man. Although he admired the fortitude and sacrifice of war, which he called "a bath of blood," he asked for "moral service" to mankind as an equal challenge. His speech on "The Moral Equivalent of War" was given at the dedication of the monument to Robert Gould Shaw, commander of the first black regiment in the Civil War.

"I Hate War"

Bernard de Bovier de Fontenelle (1657–1757), who lived to be 100, said: "I hate war: it ruins conversation."

BUCKET OF MODENA

THE OLD WOODEN BUCKET CAUSED a WAR THAT LASTED 22 YEARS!

IN 1249 A SOLDIER OF BOLOGNA DESERTED TO MODENA AND TOOK WITH HIM AN OLD HORSE WATER BUCKET WHEN MODENA REFUSED TO RETURN IT **WAR** FOLLOWED! THE RESULTING HOLOCAUST INVOLVED THE GERMAN EMPEROR AND LASTED 22 YEARS. *THE BUCKET IS STILL IN MODENA.*

ROBERT BLAKE ENGLAND'S SECOND GREATEST ADMIRAL WAS A MERCHANT AND COMPLETELY IGNORANT OF NAUTICAL MATTERS UNTIL THE AGE OF 51!

RIPLEY

3-31

Modern War Is Soft

Lord Chesterfield believed that people were getting soft in modern war and wrote to his son on January 12, 1757: "Even war is pusillanimously carried on in this degenerate age; quarter is given; towns are taken, and the people spared; even in a storm, a woman can hardly hope for the benefit of a rape."

Atilla, "The Scourge of God"

Atilla was barbarian king of the Huns in A.D. 434. According to Edward Gibbon, in his monumental *Decline and Fall of the Roman Empire,* he boasted that "the grass never grew on the spot where his horse had stood."

Atilla murdered his older brother, Bleda, with whom he had jointly ruled, and from then on there was no looking back. Twice he took the Eastern Roman Empire. The first time they paid him 700 pounds of gold a year to stay away—then he decided he would like to have the Western part. Why not? He could marry the emperor's sister, Honoria, and claim the territory as her dowry.

In 452 he invaded Italy, and ran into the pestilence raging there. It was this disease, rather than another army, which did him in. He died in 453, but it took people a long while to forget him.

Pricius, the historian, met him in 449, before he got involved with Honoria and began making his plans. He says Atilla was short and squat with a big head, a small beard, and deep-set eyes of the sort one remembers. He also noted that while Atilla's officers ate from massive silver plates they had seized as loot, Atilla himself ate from a wooden trencher. He ate only meat.

Since he was one of the most blustering figures in history, one must assume that this habit was a matter of taste rather than humility.

Dangers of the French Revolution

Sir Jonah Barrington, in his *Personal Sketches,* refers to Sir Boyle Roche as being "without exception, the most celebrated and entertaining anti-grammarian in the Irish Parliament."

A fierce patriot and fiery orator, Sir Boyle had plenty to say on the subject of war. Here is part of his famous speech on the dangers of a French invasion of Ireland:

Mr. Speaker, if we once permitted the villainous French masons to meddle with the buttresses and walls of our ancient constitution, they would never stop, nor stay, sir, till they brought the foundation stones tumbling down about the ears of the nation! . . . if those Gallican villains should invade us, sir, 'tis on *that very table,* maybe, these honourable members might see their own destinies lying in heaps on top of one another! Here perhaps, sir, the murderous Marshallawmen would break in, cut us to mince-meat and throw our bleeding heads upon that table to stare us in the face!

THE BOY WHO WAS BROUGHT BACK FROM THE DEAD BY A DOG!

JOHN GRANVILLE of Kilkhampton, England WOUNDED IN THE BATTLE OF NEWBURY AT THE AGE OF 16 AND BURIED ON THE BATTLEFIELD -- WAS DUG UP FROM HIS GRAVE BY HIS DOG AND LIVED ANOTHER 57 YEARS!

Peace, It's Wonderful!

That's what "Father Divine" used to say. But, in 1968, someone calculated that in the 3,462 years since the first recorded war in 1496 B.C., the "civilized" world had seen only 230 years of peace. Since 1968, the record seems to have worsened. Leibnitz said that the words, "here you can find perfect peace," could be written only over the gates of a cemetery.

Hurry Up and Wait

"Three-quarters of a soldier's life," said Rosenstock-Hussy, "is spent in aimlessly waiting about."

Surely an army is the only expensive thing one buys and keeps on hand, hoping it will not be needed, while constantly worrying that its existence may create a need for it.

92

The Fighting in Ireland

The history of the English in Ireland during the reign of Elizabeth I was even more violent than the bomb-racked story of Elizabeth II's reign. One massacre can serve as an example.

Walter Devereux, the queen's lord deputy for Ireland, attacked the island of Rathlin (off the coast of Antrim) in 1575. He knew that the rebellious MacDonnells had left their old, their sick, their women, and their children on the island for safety, with only a small force to guard them. The garrison offered to surrender to the English troops if they could be allowed to set sail for Scotland. This was refused, and everyone on the island—600 men, women, and children in all —was killed!

The English Longbow

The famous English longbow was invented by the Welsh and acquired by Edward I (1239–1307) during his conquest of Wales. Edward had a tendency to go back on his promises. After defeating the Welsh, he promised them a non-English-speaking leader, and then made his young son the prince of Wales. The infant could not speak English or Welsh either! He was no more reliable with his English subjects, promising that he would not collect certain taxes without the consent of Parliament and then, as they say, "welshing" on the deal.

However, he made good on his promise to English soldiers that they would never again have to go unprepared before the deadly Welsh longbows, by equipping them with an English version of the same weapon that revolutionized warfare in his country.

The NAME of the LORD!

General Lord COMBERMERE CAPTURED THE POWERFUL FORTRESS OF BHARTPUR, INDIA, IN ONE DAY — BECAUSE HIS NAME MEANT "ALLIGATOR" (IN HINDI) AND THERE WAS AN ANCIENT PROPHECY THAT THE TOWN WOULD BE CAPTURED BY AN ALLIGATOR

RIPLEY—— 2-11

"War Is Too Important To Be Left to Generals"

What Georges Clemenceau (1841–1929) really said was: "Generals cannot be trusted with anything, not even with war."

The King at the Head of His Troops

The first kings of England were war leaders elected by their fellow warriors; presiding over war councils as well as leading troops in battle was all part of their job. The last British king to actually lead his men into battle was George II. On June 27, 1743, he defeated Noailles and the French army at the Battle of Dettigen.

At Fort Necessity, the young George Washington said that he had "heard the bullets whistle; and, believe me, there is something charming in the sound." On hearing this story, King George harrumphed and, in his thick German accent, said: "He has not heard many of them or he would not think them very charming." Washington was to hear the sounds of war more and like them less, especially when he fought against this monarch's successor, George III.

Early Psychological Warfare

Tamerlane, the great Mongol conqueror, is said to have built a pyramid of 90,000 human heads before the walls of Delhi to sway that besieged city. In Christopher Marlowe's play, *Tamburlaine,* he is portrayed as using tents of different colors, to threaten worse disasters each day, if the men under his siege did not capitulate. When he won, he used the head of the conquered general as a polo ball.

Germ Warfare

Nobel Prize winner Bertrand Russell was among many who accused the United States of bacteriological warfare in the East, but there is no agreement as to how much, if any, germ warfare was practiced on either side in Korea and Vietnam.

One proven case, however, involves the British, though it dates back to 1762. At Fort Pitt in that year, blankets infested with smallpox were deliberately distributed to the Indians and helped to bring the Seven Years' War (in America, it was known as the French and Indian War) to an end. According to the terms of the Peace of Paris in February 1763, Britain got Canada, Nova Scotia, Cape Breton, St. Vincent, Tobago, Dominica, Grenada, Senegal and Minorca. France retained Martinique, Guadaloupe, St. Lucia, Goree, fishing rights off Newfoundland, and settlements in India. Britain also gained Florida from Spain, in exchange for Havana. Spain acquired Louisiana from France, while recovering Manila and the Philippines. And germ-laden blankets helped to effect all this!

TAMERLANE

THE NOTORIOUS MONGOL CONQUEROR, ON THE PRETEXT THAT HE WAS ABIDING BY THE KORAN **MASSACRED 2,000,000 MEN, WOMEN AND CHILDREN!**

BEFORE INVADING INDIA IN 1397 TAMERLANE CLOSED HIS EYES AND OPENED THE KORAN ON THIS PASSAGE: *"Prophet wage war against the intolerant and lawless"*

THE PROPHECY THAT PROVED TRUE TO THE VERY INSTANT--AFTER 5 CENTURIES!

THE TOMB OF TAMERLANE, in Samarkand, WAS OPENED BY A SOVIET SCIENTIFIC EXPEDITION AND HIS MUMMIFIED BODY WAS REMOVED AT 5 A.M. ON JUNE 22,1941 DESPITE AN INSCRIPTION ON A HUGE BLOCK OF JADE THAT READ: "IF I SHOULD BE BROUGHT BACK TO EARTH, THE GREATEST OF ALL WARS WILL ENGULF THIS LAND."

AT THE SAME MOMENT, 2,500 MILES TO THE WEST, RUSSIA WAS INVADED BY 160 GERMAN DIVISIONS AND 14,000 TANKS --EMBROILING THE SCIENTISTS' HOMELAND IN THE GREATEST OF ALL WARS!

El Supremo

Francisco Solano Lopez became a brigadier general at the age of 18. It was assumed that the president of Paraguay (whom Lopez succeeded in 1862 and who made this appointment) was his father.

Lopez was a megalomaniac who considered himself the Napoleon of South America, destined to put Paraguay on the map. In 1865 he declared war on Argentina, Brazil, and Uruguay. In this war, the War of the Triple Alliance, Paraguay lost nine-tenths of its population. Before he was finally beaten and killed in 1870, he had gained quite a reputation for fierce battle both in the field and against real or imagined enemies at home. On charges of conspiracy and treason, he had 68,200 people put to death, including his two brothers, two sisters, two brothers-in-law, and his mother.

EL SUPREMO

Francisco Solano Lopez

CAUSED MORE SUFFERING THAN ANY MAN WHO EVER LIVED!

It was said that he was greatly influenced by his Irish mistress, Eliza Lynch, whom he had met in Paris in the 1850s while trying to raise money for the building of the Paraguayan railway.

Lopez got into a lot of trouble with the United States because of an American citizen named Porter Cornelius Bliss. After minor diplomatic jobs in Brazil and Argentina, Bliss had come to Paraguay and was hired by Lopez to write a history of the country. Believing him to be engaged in spying, which the United States House Committee on Foreign Affairs later decided was a false charge, Lopez had Bliss thrown into jail and tortured for three months.

In spite of all this, Francisco Solano Lopez gained quite a reputation in South America—not, as we might suppose, for killing members of his family, or for wiping out most of his own population, but for defending the rights of little states against the tyrannies of large ones!

THE WAR BIRD!
Julius BRITTLEBANK - of Charleston, S C
HE WAS IN
CUBA WHEN THE SPANISH-AMERICAN WAR BEGAN
CHINA DURING THE 1912 REVOLUTION
MONTENEGRO AT THE OUTBREAK OF THE BALKANS, 1912
GERMANY WHEN THE WORLD WAR BEGAN
ENGLAND WHEN SHE DECLARED WAR

The STORM BIRD!

BARON KARL von WERTHER

Prussian Ambassador

WAR BROKE OUT WHEREVER HE WENT!

HE WAS AMBASSADOR TO PARIS – AND FRANCE WENT TO WAR WITH SPAIN AND ALGERIA. HE WENT AS AMBASSADOR TO DENMARK – AND THE WAR OF 1864 BROKE OUT. HE WENT TO RUSSIA AND THE CRIMEAN WAR BEGAN. HIS NEXT POST WAS VIENNA AND THE AUSTRO-PRUSSIAN WAR BEGAN. AGAIN HE WENT TO PARIS AND THE FRANCO-PRUSSIAN WAR STARTED. HIS LAST POST WAS TURKEY AND THE RUSSO-TURKISH WAR RESULTED. He was a very mild and peaceful man.

The Supreme Sacrifice

Nathan Hale (1755–1776) was a schoolteacher who served in the Revolution and who was caught spying on the British. He was executed without a trial and was recorded in American history as saying: "I only regret that I have but one life to lose for my country."

A Russian, however, went one step beyond him. When the Decemberist insurrection was broken up in Russia, Count Sporansky sentenced many conspirators to Siberia and ordered that five be quartered. The czar, however, had ordered that no blood should be shed and, on the night of July 13, 1826, the five were hanged instead. So inexperienced were the hangmen—or so heavy were the chains that bound the condemned men—that three victims snapped or escaped their ropes and plunged unharmed into the pit beneath the scaffold. When Ryleev, Muravyov-Apoostol, and Kahovsky were retrieved half an hour later for a second hanging, Ryleev is supposed to have said: "I am happy that I shall die twice for my country."

The Great de Groot

Huigh de Groot became a lawyer at the early age of 15. Under the pseudonym of Hugo Grotius, he wrote the *De Iure Belli et Pacis (Of the Law of War and Peace),* the first definitive text on international law. In 1619 he was condemned to life imprisonment, and it looked as if a promising career was over. But his wife obtained permission to join him in jail—and then smuggled him out concealed in a box of books. He died many years later from exposure after a shipwreck.

His native Holland, to which he returned in 1631 and from which he had to flee again in 1632, honored him with a statue 267 years after his death!

THE STORM THAT SETTLED A WAR
KING EDWARD III of England SIGNED THE PEACE TREATY OF BRETIGNY WITH FRANCE AFTER HIS ARMY WAS SWEPT BY HAILSTONES -CONVINCED THAT HIS IMPROPER CLAIM TO THE FRENCH THRONE HAD BROUGHT ON *A BOMBARDMENT FROM HEAVEN!*
(1360)

Good King Wenceslas' Pageboy

John Zizka (c. 1370–1474) was a bold military genius and one of the great soldiers of all time. With his use of artillery on armored wagons, he anticipated modern tank warfare by 500 years.

Born of nobility in Bohemia, he was brought up as a page to King Wenceslas, and later became royal chamberlain. He fought for the Teutonic Knights against the Poles, and for the Austrians against the Turks. He also fought for the English king, Henry V, at the Battle of Agincourt. As a commander of the Hussites, he defeated an army of King Sigismund—ten times bigger than his own—and captured Prague. Although he had lost both eyes in battle (the second at the siege of Raby, 1421), he continued to lead his men to 12 brilliant victories over Sigismund, and compelled that king to grant religious liberty to the Hussites.

During the battle at the siege of Przibislav, Zizka died of the plague. His skin was used on a drumhead, thus continuing to serve troops who carried it into battle.

The Lion of the North

Gustavus Adolphus ended the Kalmar War in 1613 by buying off the Danes, but he could also be a brave and resourceful general when fighting seemed to be the best policy. On the field at Lutzen, near Leipzig, on November 16, 1632, when his Swedish troops were greatly outnumbered by the Germans, he proved to be the most heroic of men. Leading a cavalry charge, he was shot in the arm—yet he continued. When his horse was shot out from under him, he continued on foot—until he was shot in the back. When Wallenstein's Austrian soldiers came upon him and demanded his name, this courageous man cried: "I am the king of Sweden, who seals the religion and liberty of the German nation with my blood." They fell upon him, and he died of a dozen wounds; but the sight of his battered body served only to spur his troops on. He had disciplined his army strictly and had taken stern measures against the raping, looting, and torturing that was common in those days. His men loved him and, goaded to fury by his death, they drove the Imperial troops from the field, and ended the day in victory.

THE IRON HEWERS of HISTORY

900 YRS. AGO-WILLIAM THE CONQUEROR CROSSED THE CHANNEL FROM NORMANDY AND INVADED ENGLAND

THE SOLDIER WHO STRUCK THE FIRST BLOW WAS NAMED TAILLEFER WHICH MEANS EISENHOWER

BOTH TAILLEFER AND EISENHOWER MEAN "IRON HEWER"

TAILLEFER DIED OCTOBER 14, 1066
EISENHOWER BORN OCTOBER 14, 1890

The Fighting Prophet

In one decade at Medina, Mohammed personally led 27 campaigns and raids, and planned nearly 40 more with such skill that he came to be regarded not only as the Prophet of Allah, but as one of the most able generals who ever lived.

Arthur, Once and Future King

The exploits of the semi-mythical figure, King Arthur, were first mentioned in a Welsh poem, *Gododdin,* around the year 600. In the eighth century, the historian, Nemnius, wrote of Arthur's presence at a dozen battles. By the twelfth century, Geoffrey of Monmouth was providing details of Arthur's life and his death, which he set, without hesitation, in A.D. 542 at Winchester. Later, historians, including Tennysen, in *Idylls of the King,* built Arthur into the great hero of chivalric romance.

Perhaps the most incredible tale to be told of King Arthur is in the supposedly reliable work of William of Malmesbury (1090–1143), the historian, who asks us to believe that "at Mt. Baden, relying on an image of the Virgin which he had affixed to his armor, he engaged 900 of the enemy singlehandedly and dispersed them with incredible slaughter."

Now there's a BELIEVE IT OR NOT we might find too hard to believe.

An Empire Defeated by the Weather

In A.D. 632 the Persian general, Rustam of Khurasan, led his troops across the Euphrates to Kadisiya, where he fought for four days in one of the most important battles in the history of Asia. At the beginning of the invasion, their Moslem opponents had announced themselves as "a people loving death even as thou lovest life."

This challenge, from men whose skill with the scimitar of Islam was legendary, would have been frightening enough; but, on this occasion, the Persian forces had an even greater enemy—the weather. A great sandstorm came up and blinded them while the Moslems attacked and completely wiped them out.

The brilliant career of the general was cancelled, and the whole Persian empire was defeated in a single day—by a sandstorm!

THE *BLOODLESS* HERO OF VENICE — Francesco Bussone COUNT OF CARMAGNOLA— LED THE VENETIAN ARMIES IN MORE THAN **40** BATTLES IN WHICH NOT A SINGLE MAN WAS KILLED!

The WORD IS MIGHTIER THAN THE SWORD!

THE FRENCH *GENERAL LANNES* FACING AN ENTIRE ITALIAN ARMY,
ADVANCED ALONE ON A ROAD NEAR ANCONA, AND SUDDENLY *SHOUTED*—

"HOW DARE YOU GRIP YOUR SWORDS!,
QUICK-PUT THEM BACK INTO YOUR SHEATHS!

THE ASTOUNDED ENEMY OBEYED—
— AND THE WAR WAS OVER!

The Reluctant Bishop

Will Durant, in his monumental *Story of Civilization,* notes that 3,675 churches and 425 villages in France bear the name of St. Martin. Few who honor this man's name realize that he started life as a soldier and a heathen.

Born the son of a soldier, in Pannonia, around the year 316, his father encouraged him to be a soldier too. However, Martin gave his military cloak to a beggar, and was converted to Christianity. He then went to live in a monk's cell in Italy, and later to Poitiers to be near St. Hilary. In 371, against his will, the people of Tours acclaimed him their bishop. But Martin continued to keep the strict rules of a monk, and set up a monastery at nearby Marmoutier, in which he and

80 monks lived in great austerity. Stories circulated about how he could cure the sick and raise men from the dead. His feast is Martinmas—the eleventh day of November, the day that World War I ended.

Her Beauty Killed 1,000,000 Men

If the story of Helen of Troy, with a "face that launched a thousand ships," seems spectacular, consider the woman whose beauty killed 1,000,000 men.

She was Queen Darjan, wife of Taymuraz, the king of Georgia, in the Transcaucasus. To win her hand, Abbas the Great, the emperor of Persia, started a war in 1614 that embroiled Persia, Turkey, Russia, and Georgia (now part of the U.S.S.R.). For 36 years the war raged, ending in 1650, 22 years after Abbas' death.

Hung from the Highest Yardarm

Moviegoers recall Charles Laughton as Captain Bligh of the *Bounty,* exclaiming to the mutineers that he would "see them hanging from the highest yardarm."

The last man of the British navy to be hung from a yardarm was Marine John Dalliger, on the H.M.S. *Leven,* on July 13, 1860. Oddly enough, the execution took place in China—for *attempted murders.*

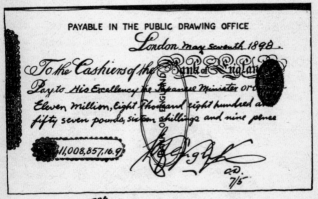

CHECK FOR $53,569,112.18 PAID TO JAPAN BY CHINA IN SETTLEMENT OF THE CHINA-JAPANESE WAR DEBT — 1898

Drinking Men's Heroes

You can learn about England's heroes by looking at that country's pub signs. In London, you can drink in history with a beer at THE ADMIRAL KEPPEL and THE ADMIRAL CODRINGTON, at THE DUKE OF GRAFTON, THE MARQUESS OF GRANBY, THE GRENADIER, JACK STRAW'S CASTLE, THE MASTER GUNNER, THE OPPORTO, and

THE PORTOBELLO. Other notable pubs include THE ROYAL OAK (in which Charles II hid after the Battle of Naseby), THE GUN (where Nelson and Lady Hamilton used to get together near the West India Docks), THE RED LION (the shield of King Arthur), and even THE WASHINGTON.

Throughout Britain, inn signs also commemorate military events: THE BATTLE OF TRAFALGAR (Portslade), THE BATTLE OF WATERLOO (Brighton), and THE BATTLE OF MINDEN (a 1759 inn at Bury St. Edmunds, where St. Edmund was buried). THE ALMA is one of the many pubs memorializing incidents of the Crimean War. There is a HEROES OF LUCKNOW (Indian Mutiny) at Aldershot, and a MAFEKING HERO (Boer War) at Bishop's Waltham. Generals from "the Great War" are represented by THE ALLENBY at Winterbourne in Zelston and THE HAIG at Hounslow. Pubs for admirals are everywhere: THE NELSON on the King's Road in Chelsea, THE BEATTY (Montsput Park), and THE JELLICOE (Canvey Island).

Some teach us fine points of history. We learn that VON ALTEN (Chatham) commanded a German legion for Britain during the Napoleonic wars. Even THE DUKE OF BRUNSWICK, who helped at Waterloo, is remembered with a pub. We learn that LEEFE ROBINSON (Harrow Weald, in Middlesex) shot down the first zeppelin at nearby Cuffey (1916). We discover that THE PLUTO, in Corby, does not refer to a planet or a Disney dog, but to the Pipeline Under the Ocean, constructed in World War II. THE RED BERET (Chelmsford) recalls the parachutists; THE GREEN BERET (Walmer) memorializes the commandos. THE DESERT RAT (Reigate) brings back memories of the North African campaign. THE JET AND WHITTLE (Podsmead) commemorates Sir Frank Whittle, pioneer in jet aircraft. WILLIE WOULD-HAVE (South Shields) invented the self-righting lifeboat in 1798. THE LADY WITH THE LAMP (Southsea) is easier to guess: it recalls Florence Nightingale, who visited the wards in the Crimea.

Even military villains are recalled. THE DUKE OF CUMBERLAND honors "The Butcher" at Culloden, who participated in the last great pitched battle in Britain. THE DUKE OF YORK, another Hanoverian princeling, was not only the second son of George III, but was also head of the army—and utterly incompetent. Equally inept was THE DUKE OF CAMBRIDGE; this grandson of George III made every member of the army contribute a day's pay to build him a monument. The column, with his statue on top, stands today in Waterloo Place, London. On top of the statue is a lightning rod. The rod was said to be the spike where the duke's creditors could file their bills. He was also the "Grand Old Duke of York," the dolt in the nursery rhyme with 10,000 men: "He marched them up the top of the hill and marched them down again." You probably remember him, and so does Britain—with a pub.

Even LORD RAGLAN, who goofed at The Charge of the Light Brigade, has a pub named after him.

But the record is probably held by the MARQUESS OF GRANBY. While one or two pubs commemorate most military heroes, he has many. The reason? It's said that when they retired, those soldiers who had served him well were given money to set up an inn. Gratefully, they named their pubs after him.

Common soldiers are honored too: THE ARTILLERY-MAN, THE RIFLEMAN, THE BRITISH VOLUNTEER. THE VOLUNTEER, at Chipping Camden, displays an old fencible on one side of the sign, a modern soldier on the other. The longest name of all may be THE THIRTEENTH MOUNTED CHESHIRE RIFLEMAN (Stalybridge). Two more are THE RECRUITING SERGEANT (Great Cornersby) and THE OLD SERGEANT (Enfield). THE

GLOUCESTERS used to depict a bewigged old member of that ancient regiment, but now exhibits a soldier of the Korean War. You'd have to be an expert to know that THE CHERRY PICKERS (Folkstone) is a military name: the nickname of the Eleventh Hussars.

Lest we forget, there are THE DISTRESSED SAILORS (Whitehaven), THE KENTISH RIFLEMAN (Dunk's Green)—which commemorates a civilian soldier of the Home Guard—and THE ROYAL MARINE (Taunton).

English pub signs, with their great sense of the past, record the story of Britain's wars over the centuries.

THE SILK WAR

SULTAN AHMED I of Turkey DECLARED WAR ON PERSIA IN 1611 BECAUSE HE COULD NOT AFFORD GIFTS FOR HIS 3,000 WIVES — AND WAS DETERMINED TO GET THEM 1,000,000 POUNDS OF SILK FROM THE PERSIANS

The Black Hole of Calcutta

In 1756, 19-year-old Siraj-ud-daula became nawab (nabob) of Bengal and broke with the British raj. He attacked Calcutta, and many of the Europeans living there sought refuge in Fort William, headquarters of the East India Company. The nawab threw 145 men and one woman into a cell because they could not lead him to the great treasure that he thought was hidden in the fort. The cell was only 18 feet by about 15 feet, with two very small windows, and it was the hot season. By the following morning, only 23 had survived!

Lord Clive retook the city in 1757, and a monument was erected over this "black hole of Calcutta" in 1902.

The Man of Destiny

Napoleon ranks as a prime literary subject. Plays were written about him by Shaw, Sardou, Moreau, Toller, Claudel, Catherwood, Caesar, Anspacher, Hasenclever, Trench, Fulop, Miller, Gregor, Raynal, and Rostand. In this respect, he ranks with Jesus Christ, Abraham Lincoln, and Shakespeare's Hamlet.

Quick March!

After the Battle of Talavera (Toledo, Spain) in the Peninsular War, a brigade under Robert Craufurd (1764–1812), which was coming to the relief of Sir Arthur Wellesley (later Duke of Wellington), marched an incredible 62 miles in just 26 hours.

Cool, Calm, and Dissected

When his arm was amputated in the field at Waterloo, Lord Raglan asked for the limb to be brought back to him so that he could remove a valuable ring from a finger. Before he could speak, he had to spit out the lead bullet he had been biting on.

Bravest Soldier in the World

François de la Noue (1531–1591), French Protestant hero in the Wars of Religion, did not want to have his bullet-shattered arm amputated during the Battle of Sainte Gemme. Not that he was afraid of the pain—for he was described as being "the bravest soldier in the world"—but he did not wish to be disfigured. Jeanne d'Albret, queen of Navarre, convinced him that the gangrenous arm should be sawed off, and she held his hand while the surgeons did it. It was replaced by an artificial arm and an iron hook, and La Noue became known as *Bras de Fer* ("Arm of Iron").

ERMENEGILDO CANALI WAS KILLED IN THE GREAT WAR BY A BOMB SPLINTER AT THE AGE OF 24 — HIS SON COSTANTINO CANALI WAS KILLED IN THE SPANISH WAR BY A BOMB SPLINTER AT THE AGE OF 24

One Bad General

Achille François Bazaine (1811–1888) was a marshal of France who ended up in jail for treason. He was really an incompetent, second only to the Emperor Napoleon III himself.

Napoleon III was dumb enough to give Bazaine supreme command of French forces in the French-Prussian War. At Metz, which was under siege for 54 days, Bazaine got into some questionable diplomatic exchanges with the Germans (designed to "save France from itself") and surrendered. After the war—the war that had driven the French to eat the animals in the Paris Zoo, and that had cost France millions in reparations (an embarrassment so stinging that her failure in both World Wars was nothing in comparison)— Bazaine was courtmartialed, convicted of treason, and sentenced to 20 years of solitary confinement.

For the first time, Marshal Bazaine finally showed some competence. He escaped and spent the rest of his life outside France.

The French have a proverb: "One bad general is better than two good ones." Where does that leave Marshal Bazaine?

Stefan Dusan

Stefan Dusan (c. 1308–1355) was also known as Stefan Uros IV after he imprisoned, strangled, and succeeded his father, Stefan Uros III. In 1346, he ordered the archbishop to crown him "czar and autocrat of the Serbs, Greeks, Bulgarians, and Albanians," and brought Serbia to the height of its power by brilliant and ruthless warfare. At his peak of glory, he took over part of Macedonia, as well as winning all of Thessaly and Epirus from the Byzantines while they were involved in other devastating wars. When Stefan decided to attack Constantinople, this ruthless and ambitious king was laid low by apparently the only enemy that could conquer him—a fever!

Abd el Kader

Abd el Kader (c. 1807–1883) frequently fought the French in Algeria, and finally declared a Holy War against them. In 1847, he was compelled to surrender when he lost the support of the sultan of Morocco after the defeat at Isly. The French imprisoned him for five years but, in 1860, they awarded him the Grand Cross of the Legion of Honor!

Famous Last Words

Everyone knows of the founder of modern nursing, the Nightingale girl who was named for her birthplace, the Italian city of Florence, and who grew up to be "the Lady with the Lamp" in the hospitals of the Crimean War.

When, on her deathbed in 1910, the 90-year-old nurse was given the prestigious Order of Merit, she simply said: "Too kind—too kind."

張獻忠

CHANG HSIEN-CHUNG

EMPEROR OF WESTERN CHINA (1644)

The BLOODY BUTCHER OF THE AGES

KILLED MORE THAN 40,000,000 PEOPLE IN 5 YEARS

Including — 32,310 students, 27,000 Buddhist Priests, 280 of his own wives,
400,000 women accompanying his army, 600,000 inhabitants of Chengtu,
and 38,000,000 inhabitants of Ssechuan.
HE DESTROYED EVERY BUILDING
IN THE COUNTRY.

The Czar Who Liked to Play Army

When Peter III of Russia (1728–1762) inherited the throne upon the death of the Empress Elizabeth, one of his first acts was to pull Russia out of the Seven Years' War, thus wasting all the efforts that Russian forces had expended in that difficult war.

In the summer of 1762, he was overthrown by a conspiracy arranged by Catherine the Great and her lover, Grigori Orlov, and his brother, Alexei. Catherine, herself—dressed in one of their uniforms—led the imperial guards and, within only a few days of her victory, Peter was assassinated by Orlov.

Peter III made no great mark in history. He was the grandson of Peter the Great, but he seems to have inherited none of the great czar's military savvy. His only interest was in playing army. Once, when a rat ran into his toy soldiers and knocked some of them down, he had the creature formally court-martialed and hanged.

"Peccavi"

Sir Charles James Napier (1782–1853) was 61 years old when he led 2,800 British troops against 30,000 Baruchis for the conquest of Sind. Recalling his schoolboy Latin, he sent a dispatch to London that simply read "Peccavi," or "I have sinned [Sind]."

THE SOLDIER WHO SERVED AS A HUMAN GUN CARRIAGE!
VALDIVIA
A MEXICAN ARTILLERYMAN IN HIS COUNTRY'S WAR AGAINST SPAIN, TO ENABLE HIS COMRADES TO ATTACK A SPANISH FORTRESS NEAR ZACATECAS, SUPPORTED A 700-LB. CANNON ON HIS BACK THROUGHOUT THE BOMBARDMENT

Honors and Awards

British Admiral of the Fleet Sir James Alexander Gordon and Rear-Admiral Sir John Hindmarsh each won the Naval General Service Medal with seven bars (a bar indicates a second award of the medal)! The first man lost a leg at the capture of the *Pomone* (1812); the second lost an eye at the Battle of the Nile (1798).

James Talbot (45th Foot) and Daniel Loochstadt (60th Foot) each won Military General Service Medals with 15 bars!

The youngest man ever to win the Victoria Cross, Britain's highest decoration, was Arthur Fitzgibbon. He was only 15 when he won it at the Taku Forts (northern China) on August 21, 1860. Years later, he was dismissed from the service for insubordination.

Oak-leaf clusters are equivalent to the British bar, indicating a repeat award. Major Clyde B. East won the American Air Medal with an incredible *42 oak-leaf clusters*.

THE ORIGINAL HEADLESS HORSEMAN
SWAN GHAZI KAMAL DECAPITATED IN COMBAT AT JHAJJAR, India, REMAINED UPRIGHT ON HIS CHARGER WHILE IT GALLOPED FROM THE BATTLEFIELD TO HIS HOME — *A DISTANCE OF 26 MILES!*

The First Congressional Medal Was Awarded to a Frenchman

The first medal awarded by the Congress of the United States was designed by a Frenchman, made in Paris, and awarded to a Frenchman.

The medal was personally presented to Lieutenant Colonel Louis de Fleury, a major of the Regiment de St. Onge, by Benjamin Franklin. Fleury, who commanded the Vanguard of the force of 11,000 men under General "Mad" Anthony Wayne, which attacked Stony Point, had dashed into the fray to strike down the British flag, thereby inspiring the revolutionary attackers.

After the brisk battle, General Wayne wrote to Washington: "The fort and garrison with Colonel Johnston are ours. Our officers and men behaved like men who are determined to be free." None was braver than Fleury. Wayne himself also received a medal from Congress for the exploit at Stony Point, but Fleury got the first—*and only*—medal of the Revolutionary War, awarded by the Americans to a foreigner.

JENGHIZ KHAN

Famous Mongolian Ruler MADE WAR UPON AND DESTROYED THE EMPIRE OF PERSIA BECAUSE—Contrary to his own habit— THE PERSIAN MONARCHS WORE THEIR MUSTACHES CURLING UPWARDS!

THE TENT OF GENGHIS KHAN, WHICH BECAME THE MONGOLIAN EMPEROR'S TOMB IN 1227, IS STILL PRESERVED IN THE MUSEUM OF EDSHEN NORO, MONGOLIA -- ALTHOUGH THE COFFIN IT SHELTERED WAS DESTROYED BY REBELLIOUS SOLDIERS

The HEAVENLY KING

HUNG HSIU-CHWAN

LEADER of the *TAIPING REBELLION* THAT COST THE LIVES
OF 50,000,000 PEOPLE —FIVE TIMES AS MANY AS FELL DURING THE WORLD WAR
AND ALL BECAUSE HE *FLUNKED* IN HIS SCHOOL EXAMINATIONS
THIS PEEVED SCHOOLBOY STARTED THE BLOODIEST MOVEMENT IN WORLD HISTORY!

The Fall of Montezuma's Empire

When Mexico fell to the Spaniards, Montezuma was no longer a ruler, and the empire no longer existed.

About 200 years before (1519), when Hernan Cortes and his comparatively few men discovered the Aztec capital at Tenochtitlan (now Mexico City), it had more than 100,000 inhabitants; and Cortes described it in a letter to his king as "the most beautiful city in the world."

Four causeways connected the 2,500-acre island (all man-made) to the mainland. They were no defense against the Spaniards, partly because Montezuma was expecting the return of the gods and thought Cortes might be "The Plumed Serpent" himself. The Aztecs therefore offered no resistance to the Spaniards, who were armed with swords, muskets, and ten artillery pieces. Eventually, the Spaniards captured and imprisoned Montezuma but, when he died, his 22-year-old nephew, Cuauhtemoc, was elected in his place, and Cortes found him much harder to handle.

Cortes beat a hasty retreat, leaving many of his men to perish. He sat down under a great tree and cried bitterly, then arose to make plans for his return. Those plans led to one of the most incredible battles of history—a naval battle 7,500 feet above sea level.

Cortes had burned his boats at Veracruz, so there could be no thought of retreat. Since he would now have to build new boats, he sent Indian runners to Veracruz to collect every bit of metal and any shred of sailcloth that remained of the old wrecks. He improvised the rest. With the assistance of 8,000 Tlaxcala Indians, traditional enemies of the Aztecs whom he had been lucky enough to recruit, Cortes carried the pieces for his 13 new brigantines over the mountains in Texcoco, where the boats were assembled.

With Tlaxcalan auxiliaries and 928 Spaniards (84 horsemen, 650 infantry, 194 crossbowmen and musketeers), Cortes attacked, dividing his forces into four groups. They simultaneously assaulted the Aztec capital from Coyocan in the south, Ixtapalapa on the southeast, Texcoco on the east, and Tacuba on the west. The siege lasted 80 days, superstition and disease being as significant as the Spanish arms in the eventual defeat. On August 13, 1521, Tenochtitlan surrendered; Hernan Cortes had brought down that high and majestic civilization in Mexico.

The soldiers despoiled the land and enslaved the people. The priests of the new religion burned the "idolatrous" records and built a church on the site of the temple to the Aztec gods. Astronomers, poets, and warriors—the Aztecs themselves—all perished.

Half-Mast

James Hall was an Englishman who led two Danish expeditions in 1605 and 1606 to Greenland. When he commanded the English expedition there in 1612, searching for the Northwest Passage, he was killed by Eskimos. In his honor, the ship *Heartsease* flew its flag at half-mast—the first recorded example of this honor to the dead.

Inspiration from the Heavens

Denmark's flag, depicting a white cross on a red field, originated with King Valdemar II, whose Christian troops attacked pagan colonies on the Baltic around A.D. 1218. The inspiration for his "Dane's cloth" *(Dannebrog)* came to him when he saw a white cross against the red background of the setting sun during battle. The vision spurred him on to success, and he later commemorated the event with what is now known to be the oldest unaltered flag design in the world.

Flags Ahoy!

Flags have played a long and colorful part in military history, and there is supposed to be nothing as "terrible as an army with banners."

The first "flags" were not pieces of cloth at all; they were solid objects, of special significance, hoisted up on a pole. Sometimes ribbons also flew from this "standard."

In ancient Egypt, four objects were carried ahead of the Pharaohs on ceremonial poles. One of them represented the king's placenta. The Assyrians and Babylonians also carried similar "magical objects" before them onto the hunting field as well as the battlefield.

An Assyrian statue of 671 B.C. shows a soldier with the standard of his military unit, and there are other representations of Assyrian standards from the ninth century before Christ.

Sometimes, as in Shakespeare's *Macbeth,* the head of an enemy, placed on a pole, served as a gruesome standard. The Greeks and Romans, however, merely used the figure of an animal, such as a bear, for their standards.

The earliest known military standard, carried by Roman legionaries, simply consisted of a sheaf of wheat tied to the end of a pole. Pliny tells us that in

THE FIRST MILITARY FLAG

The MANIPULUS—
THE EARLIEST KNOWN
MILITARY STANDARD
WAS CARRIED BY A
UNIT OF THE ROMAN
LEGION AND CONSISTED
*MERELY OF A SHEAF
OF GRAIN TIED
TO THE END OF
A POLE*

the second consulship of Gaius Marius, it was decided that the sole standard of Roman legions would be the eagle—an effigy more recently associated with Napoleon and fascist Italy, and sometimes seen perched on poles bearing the American flag. The Romans also had a cavalry flag *(vexillum)* which the historian, Livy, says was constructed of a spear with a crossbar, from which a square banner hung, thus resembling the banners now used in churches. The later Roman emperors used a similar, but larger, banner as the imperial standard *(labarum)*. At first, the banner was made from purple silk, with an eagle embroidered in gold on the cloth. Constantine introduced the *chi-rho* for Christ, and the sign of the cross: *In hoc signo vinces* ("In this sign you will conquer"). The monks of the Abbey of Marmoutier preserved the *labarum*like banner under which Clovis fought in A.D. 507. Charlemagne used a similar flag.

In China, emperors are said to have had flags carried before them on military and ceremonial occasions more than a thousand years before Christ. The flag was so closely associated with the royal person, that death was promised to any unauthorized person who touched it.

This reminds us of the unfortunate Chinese fisherman who found the long-lost skull of a long-dead emperor. He was praised for his great and valuable find, then immediately executed for having handled so sacred an object.

The Little Drummer Boy Was an Outcast

Most people know the word, "pariah," for "outcast, " (from the Tamil word *pariyar*); but few know that this is the name for the lowest caste of people in southern India, and that it comes from the word meaning "drummer." Drummers in India were considered outcasts because of their contact with the animal skins that formed their drumheads.

Military "drommes" (derived from the same word as "trumpet") have been in use since very early times. The kettledrum came from the cavalry of the Ottoman Turks, the snare drum from Swiss mercenaries. The tenor drum was used in fife and bugle bands; and the "long drum," now called the "bass drum," came to popularity in eighteenth-century England, when it was played in the "Turkish manner," with a padded stick in the right hand and a switch of birch twigs in the left.

Nature Thought of It First

Not only did ants have the first armies, but Mother Nature also thought of the following martial aids:

Airplane—aviation principles are displayed by birds, bats, and flying fish.

Parachute—a part of the anatomy of flying squirrels, milkweed, and other seeds.

Pistol—the structural part of the witch hazel that shoots out the seeds.

Sail—a natural formation on the velella, a small sea creature.

Raft—the method by which mosquitoes float their eggs on the water.

Armor—the familiar protective coverings on both the turtle and the armadillo.

Radar—an instinctive capacity of bats.

Camouflage—a phenomenon of the leaf insect, the chameleon, and a great many other creatures.

Diving Bell—a structure used by the water spider.

JUNGLE UNIFORM U.S. ARMY IS CAMOUFLAGED AND CONTAINS AN INFLATED BUOYANCY BALLOON INSIDE TO AID IN CROSSING STREAMS

GIOVANNI
GALEAZZO
(1353-1408)
COMMANDER OF THE
VENETIAN ARMY,
FOR THE CRIME OF
TREATING A DEFEATED
OPPONENT HUMANELY,
WAS ORDERED PUT TO
DEATH BY VENICE'S
GOVERNING COUNCIL
BY BEING DECORATED
WITH A GOLDEN HELMET
**THE BAND OF WHICH
HAD BEEN SOAKED
WITH POISON**

HENRY de RUVIGNY
COMMANDER
OF THE
ENGLISH

Sabotage

Everyone knows that *sabotage* means, in effect, "throwing a monkey wrench into the works." In every war, it is a very effective weapon. However, few know that sabotage originated in peace, when workers disruptively threw their wooden shoes (sabots) into the machinery.

DUKE OF BERWICK

COMMANDER OF THE FRENCH

FRENCH ARMY WITH AN ENGLISH LEADER DEFEATED AN ENGLISH ARMY WITH A FRENCH LEADER

BATTLE OF ALMANSA SPAIN 1707

Battle Cries

Henry V urged his troops to cry: *"God for England! Harry! and St. George!"*

Among the odd crys for encouraging the troops were the exasperated words of Frederick ("Old Fritz") the Great, who thundered, *"Dogs! Would you live forever?"* The battle cry that Henry Stanley's troops heard with trepidation, when they encountered the cannibals of the Congo, was *"Meat! Meat!"*

The Germans Had No Word For War

"It is a curious fact that no Germanic nation in early historic times had a word properly meaning 'war'...."

—*Oxford English Dictionary*

A Toast to Two Fighting Men

If you read sea and pirate stories as a child, you know that grog is a seafaring man's drink. It was made by diluting rum with water ("seven-water grog" is especially weak), so that the sailors would not get too drunk. Grog got its name from Admiral Edward Vernon, who diluted the sailors' drink in 1740. Vernon entered the navy at the age of 16, and fought at Gibraltar and Malaga. He commanded his own ship at age 21 and, by 24, he was a rear admiral. His capture of Portobello made him a national hero (antique collectors will have heard of Portobello Road in London). But, of course, watering their rum did not make him a hero with the fleet. He got the nickname, "Old Grog," on account of the grogham cloak he wore, and the watered rum, in turn, became "grog."

The colonel who gave his name to the landlubber's drink, *negus,* a hot and sweetened wine, was Francis Negus, who died in 1732. He was an English soldier who served under the great duke of Marlborough.

One of the strangest cases of mutiny ever recorded was one involving Private John Wilson of the 84th Yorkshire and Lancaster Regiment of the British army, whose "Act of Rebellion" consisted of a refusal to accept his daily ration of rum. At his court-martial, which took place in Bangalore, India, in November 1815, a plea for mercy was entered by claiming he had been a lifelong teetotaler. Nevertheless, he was found guilty and shot. Private Wilson lies buried in the Agram Cemetery in Bangalore, where a suitable epitaph has been inscribed on his tomb.

Peaceful

Two peaceful phrases that have come into common American usage originated in war dispatches. "All quiet on the Potomac" was used often by General McClellan during the Civil War. "All quiet on the Western Front" was used in periods of calm during the trench warfare of World War I.

ALFRED McCOY
WAS A 1ST CLASSMAN
IN ANNAPOLIS
AT THE SAME TIME
HIS SON WAS 4TH CLASSMAN IN WEST POINT

Stubborn As a Shavetail

It has been suggested that the nickname, "Shavetail," for a second lieutenant in the army, came about when a West Point cadet donned the regular army uniform at graduation. Thus, his coattails, in effect, had been "shaved off."

But the word is actually associated with the animal world, not the military. In the late nineteenth century, a young and unbroken mule was called a "shavetail." So, it was natural that an untried officer, a new second lieutenant, would be compared to that untrained and untested beast.

Slush Fund

Sailors called the fat and grease refuse from the galley "slush" and, at one time, it was used to "slush" ships' masts and spars.

The term "slush fund," usually associated with politics, originated when the British navy allowed warships to sell the slush and other refuse for money to be divided among the enlisted men.

In time, "slush" came to mean all unwanted equipment, worn-out "government-issue" materials, and effects left by deserters. The "slush fund" was the money raised by its sale.

THE INDESTRUCTIBLE MAN!
SGT. NICHOLAS RIGOPOULOS
SHOT 9 TIMES THRU THE HEAD - STILL LIVES!
HE WAS CAPTURED BY THE COMMUNISTS IN PARNASSIS, GREECE, AND SHOT BY A FIRING SQUAD - LATER HE WAS FOUND TO BE STILL ALIVE AND WAS EXECUTED A SECOND TIME! — AND AGAIN A THIRD TIME — BUT WITH 9 BULLETS THRU HIS HEAD HE WALKED 2 MILES TO A VILLAGE AND WAS RESCUED

A Martin, a Mouse, and a Male Chauvinist Pig

Military men have always liked French words: *liaison, debacle, revetment, surveillance, reconnaissance, reveille*—the list seems endless. Two interesting French words enshrine a pair of fascinating Frenchmen: Martinet and Chauvin.

A frequently wounded veteran who never tired of relating stories about his beloved commander's (Napoleon) triumphs was Nicholas Chauvin of Rochfort. He gave us the word, *"chauvinism."*

Jean Martinet was a very strict lieutenant colonel and inspector general of infantry under Louis XIV. His last name became synonymous with any excessively

138

strict disciplinarian, or a nit-picking military man. Martinet suffered a humiliating death: he was shot by his own men when he got too far ahead of the artillery, while leading an infantry charge at Duisberg in 1672. A Swiss captain, Soury (pronounced the same as *souris,* the French word for "mouse"), was killed by that same volley, and at the time, some army jokers said that this battle "cost the king only a Martin and a Mouse."

THE MOST INTREPID SOLDIER IN HISTORY!
GENERAL JEAN-BAPTISTE SOURD
(1775-1849) of France
HAD HIS RIGHT ARM AMPUTATED IN THE FIELD DURING THE BATTLE OF WATERLOO
- YET HE WAS AGAIN LEADING HIS TROOPS ONLY ONE HOUR LATER!
June 18, 1815

And "Nuts" To You **Too,** Freddy!

In modern warfare, generals have responded to unacceptable messages as briefly as "nuts" and "merde." The latter was translated in the history books as: "The Old Guard dies, but never surrenders."

The cavalry genius von Seydlitz was somewhat less terse but considerably more witty when Frederick the Great ordered him to charge the still-unbroken Russian infantry at the Battle of Zorndoff in 1758: "Tell His Majesty that my head will be at his disposal after the battle, but that as long as the battle lasts, I intend to use it in his service."

Prince William of Gloucester

Prince William was the son of the duke of Gloucester, and the nephew of George IV. He entered the British army with the rank of colonel of the First Foot Guards at the age of 13, and was a major-general by the age of 20. He received his master of arts degree from Cambridge at the age of 15 as a result of similar favoritism. Christopher Hibbert, who wrote the biography, *George IV: Prince of Wales,* was not impressed. Of Prince William, he simply said: "His intellectual powers were severely limited."

THE YOUNGEST SOLDIER IN ALL HISTORY! BABY WILLIAM, IN THE BATTLE OF NORTHALLERTON, ENGLAND, RODE INTO THE FRAY STRAPPED IN A CRADLE LASHED TO THE SADDLE OF HIS FATHER, THE EARL OF ALBEMARLE -- AT THE AGE OF 8 MONTHS! THE ENGLISH LOST ONLY THEIR COMMANDER, GILBERT de LACY, IN THE BATTLE, BUT 11,000 OF THE SCOTTISH INVADERS WERE KILLED! OCT. 22, 1138

Ochterloney of India, Rumford of Europe

Sir David Ochterloney, masterly military mind, baronet, and Knight Grand Cross of the Order of the Bath, entered the Bengal army in 1777 and, by 1814, he was a major-general. He reorganized the government of central India, conducted brilliant campaigns, and conquered Nepal.

Another man, Sir Benjamin Thompson (1753–1814) had something in common with Sir David. When the American Revolution broke out, Thompson abandoned his post as major in the New Hampshire Regiment and went to England, leaving his wife and baby in America. He was a scientist, elected to the Royal Society,

141

but he found time to fight the Americans as a lieutenant colonel of the king's forces, and was knighted after the Revolution.

From England, he went off to reform the armies of Bavaria and was made minister of war in that country. In his spare time, he designed the "English Garden" in Munich, dabbled with experiments in heat and light, and invented a few things, including the Rumford stove. He became president of the Council of Regents and governed Bavaria, serving also as a generalissimo for the armed forces.

In 1776 he left the service, after having won many decorations, and went to Paris where, in 1804, he married the widow of another scientist, the genius of chemistry, Antoinne Lavoisier. He died a decade later, as a count of the Holy Roman Empire, in the villa at Auteuil. Even in his later years, he was still involved with scientific experiments, and was famous worldwide.

What, you might well ask, did these two extraordinary men have in common besides their military success? *They were both born in Massachusetts;* Ochterloney in Boston, Thompson in Woburn.

First Jet Planes

Germany flew the first jet plane before World War II. It was piloted by Flug-Kapitan Erich Warsitz at Marienehe on August 27, 1939, and was powered by a Heinkel turbojet engine which had been tested two years before. The British did not get a jet into the air until May 15, 1941—and then only for a period of 17 minutes.

Jet propulsion had been suggested by Captain Marconnet as early as 1909, turbojets as early as 1921 by Maxime Guillaume.

"TIGER" A CANNON, IS PRESERVED in the Canary Islands

AS A MEMORIAL TO BRITAIN'S INABILITY TO CAPTURE THE ISLAND OF TENERIFFE BECAUSE IT BLEW OFF ADMIRAL NELSON'S RIGHT ARM (July 25, 1797)

ROMAN SOLDIERS
FORMED A DEFENSIVE CIRCLE SO STAUNCH
THAT THEIR MASSED SHIELDS COULD SUPPORT
THE IMPACT OF CHARGING CHARIOTS!

IN MILITARY DRILLS THEY OFTEN
PERMITTED HORSES TO PULL CHARIOTS
OVER THE TOP OF THE FORMATION

The Bloody Tower

An old music-hall song tells of the ghost of Anne Boleyn walking the corridors of the Tower of London "with 'er 'ead tucked underneath 'er harm."

The Tower was established by Julius Caesar, but the most prominent building still standing was built in 1078 by Bishop Gundulf of Rochester. The very medieval exterior was created for the Tower by Sir Christopher Wren (1632–1723). Part of the north bastion was destroyed by air raids in 1940, but most of the 13-acre complex, with all its memories of dark deeds and famous prisoners, remains. Queen Elizabeth escaped from the tower and lived to send her own enemies there; Sir Thomas More had his head chopped off there (though he asked the headsman to spare his beard) as did the wives of Henry VIII, Anne Boleyn and Catherine Howard.

With so many deaths in its history, one section came to be known as the "Bloody Tower" and another as the "Traitors' Gate." There are many tales of ghosts haunting the precincts, and at least one of these stories has stood up in court.

John Patto, of the King's Royal Rifles, was court-martialed in 1864 on charges of sleeping during guard duty at the Tower. He avoided the firing squad by swearing that he had challenged a ghostly figure and had lunged at it with his bayonet—which, in the best ghostly tradition, passed clean through the grisly apparition. His argument was that he was not sleeping but had been knocked unconscious by the ghost.

Two unimpeachable witnesses confirmed his story, and Patto went free when they testified under oath that they had seen the same ghost.

THE SENTRY WHO WAS SAVED BY A GHOST !

The British, The Americans, The Germans and a Pig

In 1873, German Emperor Wilhelm I decided that the island of San Juan, near Vancouver, Canada, belonged to the United States. The emperor was called in to arbitrate a dispute between Britain and the United States which, it was feared, would lead to war. The British fleet was there, ready for battle, and so were American forces, under General Winfield Scott.

The problem, of course, was who owned the island of San Juan? The bitterness started with an official of the Hudson Bay Company and an American farmer named Layman Culver. It seems that the Canadian—though this territory was not, at the time, strictly part of Canada—owned a pig that wandered onto Culver's farm. Culver shot it. But the question of San Juan ownership was still not resolved.

So, a pig almost started a war between Britain and the United States—and a German emperor had to settle the matter.

I Didn't Catch the Name

The Battle of Sadowa (1866) is also known as both the Battle of Koniggratz and the Battle of Hradoc Kralove.

THE MOST MODEST WARRIOR
IN THE HISTORY OF FRANCE
Jean Louis Reynier (1771-1814)
IN 1794 WAS TWICE APPOINTED A
GENERAL IN THE FRENCH ARMY,
BUT BOTH TIMES REFUSED TO
ACCEPT THE PROMOTION
-INSISTING HE WAS TOO
YOUNG AND INEXPERIENCED-

5 YEARS LATER HE AGREED TO
BECOME A GENERAL AND PROVED
TO BE ONE OF NAPOLEON'S
ABLEST MILITARY LEADERS

A Standing Army

The founding fathers of the United States ("a republic," said Benjamin Franklin, "if you can keep it") were strongly opposed to it having a standing army. They disbanded the Continental Army within six months of the end of the war. They also disbanded the Navy and the Marines.

Today the Republic still stands, but its biggest expense each year is keeping up its standing army.

No Hard Feelings

General Charles Cornwallis, who surrendered to Washington at Yorktown in 1781, went on to become a marquess and a hero.

He was made governor-general and commander-in-chief of Bengal, where he defeated Tippoo Sahib, a fierce rajah whose favorite plaything was a near-life-size toy tiger that, when wound up, emitted growls and appeared to devour a British soldier.

In Ireland, Cornwallis sternly suppressed the rebellion that broke out in 1798. Then he helped to negotiate the Treaty of Amiens which, for a time, quieted Napoleon. For a second time, he was appointed governor-general of India and died on his way up the Ganges to suppress still another rebellion against the British.

Thus ended a career that the British Parliament once described as full of "brilliant successes"—apparently with no hard feelings about that unlucky time at Yorktown.

Laos-y Luck

One-half of the entire Royal Laotian Air Force, which consisted of ten planes in 1965, was destroyed when a machine gun went off accidentally.

He Invented The Ambulance

Dominique Jean Larrey (1766–1842), while surgeon-general of Napoleon's army, introduced *ambulances volants* (1792), precursors of modern ambulances.

William Eaton and the Barbary Pirates

William Eaton was born in Woodstock, Connecticut, in 1764, and graduated from Dartmouth College. After serving in the American Revolution and the Indian wars in Ohio, he was sent to Tunis, in 1798—as American consul, a post that needed a military man, since the Barbary Coast had one overriding problem: pirates.

He came back to the United States in 1804 with a bold plan: support Hamet Karamanli, claimant to the throne of Tripoli, and overthrow the regime that was supporting the Barbary pirates. Congress, with some reluctance, appointed him "navy agent" to the Barbary states (Tripoli, Tunis, Algeria, and Morocco), hoping that somehow he could eliminate the costly depridations of these corsairs who ravaged the Mediterranean coastal towns and engaged in piracy and slave-trading.

In Egypt, Eaton persuaded Karamanli to undertake the venture. He borrowed $20,000 and put together a motley group of men for the assault. Believing the only way to attack Tripolitania was from the land side, he marched this ragtag army 600 miles across the desert, attacked from the rear, and captured the city of Derna.

Despite this valiant effort, Eaton was deprived of all the glory because John Rodgers had meanwhile succeeded—where everyone else had failed—in simply talking the Barbary pirates into ceasing their attacks on United States ships.

WILLIAM EATON
AMERICAN CONSUL
IN TUNIS

The LADY ADMIRAL
—
LASKARINA
BOUBOULINA
of Greece
COMMANDED
HER OWN
FLEET
IN A
4-YEAR WAR
AGAINST
THE TURKS!
(1821-1825)

ADMIRAL EDWARD RUSSELL
(1653-1727)
ACCEPTED A $100,000 BRIBE
FROM KING LOUIS XIV OF FRANCE
THEN FORWARDED THE MONEY
TO KING WILLIAM III OF ENGLAND
AND FOUGHT THE BATTLE
OF LA HOGUE
- ONE OF THE OUTSTANDING
BRITISH NAVAL VICTORIES
OF HISTORY

High Cost of Peace

In 1974—a year in which the United States was not engaged in warfare (although America has been involved in over 100 wars throughout her history)— every man, woman, and child in the country contributed $375 to military expenditures.

Clean Up, Paint Up

In 1965, East German officials launched a "beautification" campaign to fix up the Berlin Wall. The idea was "to make it appealing."

Keeping Watch

In 1802, municipal authorities of Rye, on the English coast, hired an armed sentry to keep watch for a Napoleonic invasion. The last man in the job was "Chummy" Barton. The job had been handed down in his family since 1802. "Chummy" died in 1944, and the city council called off the watch—123 years after the death of Napoleon.

Remembrance Day

After he was dead, the body of Oliver Cromwell, the Lord Protector, was dug up, and his head was used as a football in Westminster Hall. Since that incident, an English clergyman kept Cromwell's head, refusing to return it to the "authorities" because of the indignities that it had suffered earlier.

The wooden leg of Santa Anna, the famous Mexican general, was used as a baseball bat by American soldiers. The leg was last known to be in Memorial Hall, located in Springfield, Ohio.

Safety First

The National Safety Council states that an ammunition plant is one of the safest places one can work. Your own home holds more chance of being the site of an explosion.

The Pioneers' Monument

At Newgrange, the Bronze Age's burial place of the High Kings of Tara in ancient Ireland, a tomb was designed in such a way that each year on a certain day, the sun would shine along a long corridor and strike the altar deep within the man-made hill.

The Greeks likewise constructed certain temples so that a shaft of light would come from a hole artfully placed in the roof of a temple to light the face of certain statues.

In Pretoria, South Africa, there is a Pioneers' Battle Monument; and it, too, is constructed so that each year, on December 16th (the anniversary of a battle), a ray of light enters its dome and illuminates the memorial stone.

An Epitaph

The wars that have raged throughout history have claimed innumerable victims, and some of the fallen soldiers have been honored with touching or curious epitaphs. From the hundreds that we have seen on gravestones all over the world, we have chosen this one as the most unique:

In Memory of
THOMAS THETCHER
a Grenadier in the North Reg't. of Hants Militia,
who died of a violent fever contracted by drinking
Small Beer when hot, the 12th of May 1764.
Aged 26 years.
In grateful remembrance of whose universal good-
will towards his Comrades this Stone is placed
here at their expense as a small testimony of their
regret and concern.
Here sleeps in peace a Hampshire Grenadier
Who caught his death by drinking cold Small Beer.
Soldiers be wise from his untimely fall
And when ye're hot, drink Strong or none at all.

In 1781, the officers of the North Regiment of Hampshire Grenadiers restored the monument, after it had
"decay'd," and added a couplet to the above admoni-
tion:

An honest Soldier is never forgot
Whether he die by Musket or by Pot.

To this day, you can see Thomas Thetcher's epitaph
on a gravestone in front of Winchester Cathedral.

WAITING FOR FURTHER ORDERS

SOLDIER'S GRAVE IN TIOGA CO., PENNSYLVANIA